SUCCESSFUL RETIREMENT

Edited by
Norman Wright

Design: Graham Rees
Illustrations: Robert Broomfield

Choice Publishing Limited
First Floor, 2 King Street
Peterborough PE1 1LT

© Choice Publishing Ltd
Published under licence for ©Bayard Presse (UK) Limited 2008

ISBN 0 9537274 8 3
Whilst every care has been taken in the preparation of material to ensure the accuracy of Successful Retirement, Choice Publishing Ltd., & Bayard Presse (UK) Ltd., can accept no responsibility for the consequences of actions based on the advice contained herein.
Readers are urged to seek relevant professional advice based on their personal circumstances.

Contents

Chapter		Page
1	Introduction	5
2	Retire now or later?	9
3	Early retirement	15
4	Your pension explained	23
5	State benefits and your rights	35
6	Your perks	51
7	Tax when you're retired	55
8	Your savings	65
9	Moving on or staying put	79
10	Sorting out your affairs	89
11	All in a good cause	99
12	Staying fit and feeling good	107
13	Good service	117
14	Useful information/helplines	129

Chapter one

INTRODUCTION

Make the most of the good times ahead

NOWADAYS most of us are looking forward to a new phase of our lives when we "retire". Unlike our parents we have a huge range of possibilities as well as just taking it easy ahead of us. But like everything else, a little preparation goes a long way. It will ensure that you do keep fit, enjoy a happy home-life and have enough income to live comfortably, maybe to start a new career, to follow your hobbies and to take some well-earned holidays.

Even if you haven't yet given your retirement a passing thought, with our help it's not too late to start.

More than 40% of the country's adults are aged 50 or over and are likely to be much better off than previous generations.

Increased leisure means much more time for healthy exercise. On top of this are the sensible diets more and more families have already switched to and, just as important, a change of attitude to welcome the opportunities now opening for you.

Boredom and a dull life will certainly never be on the agenda.

MAKING IT WORK

OF COURSE none of this will just happen overnight. And if you are about to enter this lifestage, then making the most of the exciting times ahead will mean being quite sure about the money you have, the help you may be entitled to from the State as well as knowing how to get the most from your savings and what you should do to best look after your health.

Ever-changing rules and regulations often make modern living seem very confusing. It's all too easy, for instance, to miss out on something that is yours by right simply because the form you were asked to fill in didn't make sense. Knowing your rights is one thing, actually getting them is quite another.

Changes in interest rates, income tax and inflation can all make deciding what to do with any savings a real headache. Then there's the probability of having to budget on a smaller income, and coping with the endless offers of financial "help" that you'll get the minute you retire.

TIMING IT RIGHT

THE key to a successful retirement is planning...and this guide will show you how, whether you have decided to work through until the official State retirement age or are considering, like so many others today, whether to go early.

It explains some of the important recent changes affecting pensioners, including all the latest Budget changes.

In addition the book has at-a-glance tax tables, a section on State Benefits, your basic consumer and public rights plus lots of advice on how to stay in tip-top condition.

You'll want to keep details of your pension, insurance details and other personal commitments. Use the chart on page 143 as an easy reference list.

Now read on...you can be sure you are in good hands!

Chapter two

RETIRE NOW OR LATER

Getting your timing right

WORKING out when is the best time to retire isn't easy. If you have always hated your job, or the commuting it involves, you may want to go as soon as possible and will leap at any offers of early retirement.

The chances are you will want to tackle something new. A growing number of people don't actually retire. They may leave one job but then start working part-time locally instead, or even get the business they have always dreamed about finally off the ground.

So it all depends on what you actually mean by retirement.

At the moment the State Pension age is women for 60 and men for 65, but this will gradually change and in anyone born 1955 or after will retire at 65 this will increase until (at the moment) the retirement age is 68. Many can retire earlier and receive their occupational pension others can carry on this is dependent on their occupation and company policy.

But for the vast majority of people, retirement still means giving up the job you have held for years and taking whatever State and employer's pension you are entitled to, perhaps working a little "on the side" to supplement what is probably a lower income.

After you reach State pension age you can work and keep your earnings without your State Pension being affected – although you will be liable for tax!

Even so, before you can do this with any kind of confidence, you need to be sure exactly what money you are going to be entitled to, as well as any benefits you may also be able to claim.

All this can make the difference between whether you should

retire now or later. Even before calculating your finances, consider your health. It will be your greatest asset in retirement, so don't do anything to jeopardise it.

There are so many other things to consider too...those who are lucky enough to have a company car, for instance, will have to hand it back and this could mean having to buy one to replace it or investigating what kind of concessions – if any – are offered on local public transport.

Some employers give company car drivers the chance to buy their car at retirement at an advantageous price, an option worth considering. If it guzzles too much petrol for private motoring, or would cost too much to insure or service, don't reject the offer out of hand. Shop around local car dealers to see if they would give you a good trade in price for one which suits you better. And be sure to choose a car which can be serviced and repaired locally.

CARRY ON EARNING

SINCE October 1989, when the Earnings Rule was abolished, you have been able to earn what you want and claim your State Pension in full without it being affected, at £90.70 (single) or £145.05 (couple).

However, any earnings, pension(s) and interest on savings will be subject to tax once your income goes above your Personal Allowances each year (see page 130).

This could be important if you plan to work for a bit longer but in a different capacity, or even in the same job. Instead of putting off claiming your State Pension until you finally leave the company, you can now carry on working *and* claim your State pension.

However, if you opt to carry on working in your present job for a further five years you may choose not to claim your State Pension immediately. If you defer it, it will increase your pension each year for a maximum of five years, alternatively this can be taken as a lump sum. However, with the exception of the increases that can be claimed by your Estate, you will lose it all if you die in the meantime.

But deferring your State Pension is not cost effective – you would have to receive it for an extra 13 years or so before recouping what you gave up!

Also, if you are a married man, your wife would not be able to claim any pension based on your contributions until you started to collect yours. If she has built up a right to a State Pension through her own N I contributions (not the "Small stamp" that married women were able to opt for), she will receive it when she reaches retirement age.

Once you reach State pension age, you shouldn't have to make any more National Insurance contributions.

So is carrying on working a good idea? only you can decide of course. But it can certainly make sense if your boss is willing to continue to employ you at the same wage and under the same conditions, if you are in good health and if your take-home pay is considerably higher than the basic State Pension.

For men, there is one major disadvantage in deferring your State Pension – it deprives your wife of claiming a pension based on your N I contributions.

MAKING YOUR DECISION

SO HOW can can you decide what's best for you? One way is to write down all your options. To do this properly you will have to finish reading this book of course – but if you have a notebook ready you can jot down the relevant bits as you go through the various sections.

And to help you work all this out there's a useful budget planner on page 77 you can fill in to help you make these calculations.

First of all list your present "income"... that's your earnings at work and from any investments or savings you may have.

What would replace this if you gave up your job?

You might get a pension from your employer, for instance, but you could miss out here by claiming too early... see Chapter Four.

Then write down what your income would be if you retire at the "official" time. Last but not least calculate what would happen if you put off your retirement.

To help you make these calculations, the DSS (now renamed THE DEPARTMENT OF WORK & PENSIONS) offers a special forecasting service about what State Pension you will get depending on exactly when you decide to retire. Ask for Form BR19 at your local DWP Benefits Agency.

At first glance, the form you are asked to fill in does look a bit complicated but in fact it is very straightforward – though the reply you get back may not be!

You'll soon find that your life becomes an open book to the authorities, so resign yourself to declaring your details to all and sundry, from the DWP to the administrators of former pension schemes. Now is the time to have records at your finger-tips – National Insurance numbers for you and your spouse, income details such as P60 forms, certificates of birth, marriage, divorce (if that applies to either of you), and death of your spouse if you are widowed, and dates of any periods when you have worked abroad.

You'll also want to chase up any former pensions due from ex-employers. If they have moved, merged, changed their name or gone out of business, your Scheme funds should still be safe (with one or two scandalous exceptions!). To track them down, write to:

The Registry of Pension Schemes, PO Box 1NN, Newcastle-upon-Tyne, NE99 1NN.

Once you have a clear picture of your money situation, you need to work out your outgoings – and whether these will change once you stop working. Heating bills will increase, for example, if you are home more, but you may well save on travel costs.

And this may be just as true if you decide to take some kind of part-time job locally – in fact you might find you are actually better off than now simply because your outgoings are so much less even though your earnings are reduced.

Only when you have worked all this out can you make your final decision. But the most important point of all is that it should be your choice when you finally decide to retire. At the end of the day it is much better to retire voluntarily than to feel forced in some way.

Switch to something else for a real challenge – after all, a change is as good as a rest! If you have the good health and financial stability to choose this course, start planning now – you don't suddenly want to find yourself in a position where you don't have any options.

On the other hand it's also a fact that many retired people carry on putting away lots of money "for a rainy day" when in fact they could be enjoying some of it now.

Others feel obliged to skimp and save in order to leave an inheritance for children who probably are in fact better-heeled than their parents. What matters is to get the balance right.

Once you have worked out your cash situation for all the choices open to you, then you want to make sure too that there will be no chance of boredom and loneliness ruining any of your ideas. The secret is to be realistic about just what will replace the hours of work you have been putting in every day.

Plan meticulously for the better things in life...you deserve them! Then put in your notice at whatever age you finally decide to call it a day, making sure that you have a very good idea about just how you are going to be spending all that wonderful free time you will have on your hands!

Once people know locally that you are retired, you will be inundated with requests to help, drive, collect for charity, run a Scout troop, edit a newsletter...

If you decide to catch up on some education you missed, check for courses at your local adult education centre, regional college or one of the organisations on page 141.

Chapter three
EARLY RETIREMENT
Facts to help you choose

THESE days more and more people are opting to go early. One reason is that they are much better off than previous generations, but in addition they have a very different attitude.

Today life is to be enjoyed and for more and more of us that does not mean sitting in a long traffic jam on the way to work every day, fighting for a seat on the train or staying at the workbench or desk.

By 50 or so, lots of us are beginning to get tired of all this hassle. If you are in this age group you may well have finished paying off your mortgage – and even if you haven't, your house should be worth more than when you bought it.

You may have inherited a bit of money or made one or two good investments. And on top of all this you could have put sufficient into your company pension fund to get a decent sum.

All these things may well make you decide to launch into something new. It's worth noting that there are now loans, Government grants and finance available if your "retirement" plan is to run a business of your own.

As an employee you may well have been cotton-woolled against the harder facts of business life. You will probably have had few direct dealings with the tax man. Your salary cheque arrives on time each month.

Take the plunge to become self-employed and all this will change – and often not entirely for the better, certainly to begin with anyway. You need to budget for this carefully – and get expert help.

Unless you are really ambitious and can call on business expertise, you are better not borrowing to set up in self-employment. If you must use a loan to start you off, all the major High Street banks now have active small business sections. They can also give you details of a very wide range of other grants. Try to negotiate for free banking for the first year.

Remember, though, that if you are not impressed with your own particular branch you have the right to change banks. Today's competition among the big banks is pretty cut-throat and shopping around can really pay.

WHEN THERE'S NO CHOICE

FOR some early retirers it isn't choice that makes them go...it's redundancy. There's no doubt that to be made redundant at 50 or 55 after a lifetime of loyal service can be a catastrophic experience. But for lots of people it really is a new beginning – and years later they are pleased it happened.

All the evidence shows that many people made redundant after a long period of service do much better afterwards than they ever did in their traditional workplace.

However, in a situation like this it's important to take advice – from your firm's counsellors, for example, who in any large-scale redundancy programme should be called in to help you.

If you find yourself in this situation, much will depend of course on the size of any redundancy payment you get. As a rule it will be based on the number of years' service you have put in...certainly this is the case for the minimum State provision.

The minimum redundancy sum your employer must give is one week's pay for every year worked between age 22 and 40, plus one-and-a-half week's pay for every year over the age of 41, to a maximum limit. A generous employer could give more.

Payment is limited to your 20 years most recent service. Earlier years do not count.

From April 2005 employers no longer have the right to insist that you take retirement at state retirement age. You can still begin to take State Pension and continue to work or defer it which earns you extra pension, or a lump sum, when you do take it. You don't have to pay tax on a redundancy payment under £30,000. But however much you get, the most important step you can take is not to do anything until you have expert help.

If your company hasn't brought in anyone to help you here then make sure the kind of advice you get is independent. Your Citizens Advice Bureau – address in the phone book – is a good starting point if you do not already have an independent financial adviser.

In the meantime put the money somewhere safe to earn interest. Don't touch it till you are quite sure you know what your plans are.

It's also important to sign on at your Unemployment Benefit Office, not just to draw Jobseekers Allowance that you are entitled to but also to help safeguard your State Retirement Pension for the future. While you are claiming Jobseekers Allowance, and genuinely seeking work, your National Insurance contributions that go towards your State Pension are credited and you won't miss out.

However, the amount of your occupational pension will be set against any benefit you may be allowed, and your Jobseekers Allowance will be reduced by 10p for every 10p of any occupational pension over £50, except that the first £50 is ignored while you are in receipt of the Contributions based allowance (ie, the first six months).

Bear in mind Jobseekers Allowance will stop at the age of 60 for women, 65 for men.

It may be that instead of going to work for another employer you decide to use your redundancy pay to set up something on your own. Many of the most successful small businesses in recent years have been founded on redundancy.

JOB-HUNTING

FOR THE best chance of success, you have to spread your net as wide as possible. Let family, friends and former colleagues know that you are available – most jobs are never advertised, they are filled internally or through contacts.

Looking for a job is a full-time job in itself and needs the same number of hours and personal discipline to stick to a proper working day. If you are looking for work in the same line of business, you are at your most valuable just after you leave your job, when your contacts are freshest and your experience and knowledge bang up to date.

You have only 40 working hours a week to look for a paying job. Despite all the temptations to relax, if you watch TV or spend too long at the pub at lunchtime, you are only cheating yourself of the chance to beat the competition and get a worthwhile job.

It's going to be tedious and often disappointing – research shows that you may need to apply for up to 100 jobs to get 10 interviews to be offered a single job. But, experience shows that persistence pays. Scan local newspapers and trade magazines, not just for job adverts, but also for news of local businesses starting up or expanding which could create suitable openings.

The possibilities at this stage are limitless. You could offer your experience and contacts to a company in a similar line of business to the one you are now leaving.

Alternatively, register with the Job Centre and staff agencies, if you are going for the sort of post which asks for a CV (short for Curriculum Vitae, a summary of your personal details, qualifications and work experience), make it relevant to the job in question.

Employers are only interested in what you can do for their

enterprise, so stress how much YOUR experience can help THEM.

Don't reject any opportunities until you are in a position to make a choice. If you are given an interview, find out about the company before you go to see them.

The Department of Works and Pensions funds programme centres run by outside organisations. However you do not have to go to the local Jobcentre Plus, you can ring Jobseeker Direct on 0845 6060234.

YOUR PENSION ENTITLEMENT

LOTS of people who want to retire early get confused about what pension they will get. The answer is that regardless of what your private pension arrangements are, early retirement does not entitle you to the State Pension yet.

You will not be able to claim this until you reach the official pension age. And you would need to check the situation regarding contributions should you retire earlier than this, to make sure you could still get the full amount when you reach the "official" age.

An occupational pension over £50 counts as income and can adversely affect whatever Jobseekers Allowance you might receive, but it may still be worth signing on as unemployed. Others may be forced to retire early through ill-health when they will get Incapacity Benefit. This is payable right away.

Tax rules on occupational pension schemes or company pensions have become more complicated in recent years, but the 1989 Budget may have helped some of those who wanted to retire early.

Basically, what happened then was that the relief given to the self-employed which allowed them to take their personal pension savings at any age after 50 was, in part, extended to employees. A maximum of two-thirds final salary may now be paid in pension on retirement between 50 (55 from 2010) and 70, though to qualify you must have been with the same employer for 20 years.

But the reality is probably nowhere near as generous to employees below top management level and will depend on individual schemes and their provisions.

There have also been changes to the tax-free lump sum provision within some company schemes. You can now sometimes take a lump sum of up to 25% of your total pension fund.

This is a maximum allowed. Each individual scheme can set their own limit providing it doesn't exceed 25%. Many schemes previously operated a maximum of one-and-a-half times final salary and they may continue this policy. From 2010 the earliest retirement age will increse from 50 to 55 although schemes can introduce this rule now.

This could mean that more cash is available to you at a younger age, when you can probably put it to better use – setting up a business, for instance. But not every scheme offers this chance.

All this makes early retirement dependent on the rules of your company scheme... or how much you have managed to put into your personal pension. Government regulations mean you can't have a refund from previous employers' schemes after you have put in two years' pensionable service.

Safeguarding your lifestyle

THERE'S one thing anyone retiring early will soon notice – the major difference between work and retirement is the end of those annual rises which kept you at least in step with inflation.

Once you are retired you will be very much at the mercy of inflation. Even though your State Pension is index-linked and will rise each year, this rise is linked to the previous year's inflation rate.

In addition, an occupational pension, based as it is on what the employer is prepared to provide, is far less likely to be fully index-linked and may become less in real terms the longer you draw it. And the earlier you start the sooner you are likely to notice this.

You need to get good independent financial advice on how best to safeguard your position. You could consider putting some of your money into a tax-free ISA, where you pay no tax on savings.

There's more about all this in the "Your Savings" chapter. But whatever you do, try to resist the understandable temptation to pay off all your financial obligations and then live on basic income.

Instead, make what money you have work actively for you in

retirement since you will have fewer chances of making additional income – and this can apply even if you take this step early.

SHOULD YOU PAY UP?

AND what about paying off your mortgage? Using redundancy money for this could well be a mistake, especially if you then start working again. However, if you are retiring nearer the 'official' age and not planning to carry on working more than part-time, using a pension lump sum to pay off your mortgage can sometimes makes sense. This is particularly so, if mortgage rates are high. High mortgage rates make it more difficult to find alternative investments that will earn enough to cover the cost of the interest you are paying.

The answer depends on the mortgage interest rate in force at the time, at the moment mortgage rates are at a historic low.

Instead of actually paying off your mortgage, you could use any lump sum to improve your home, looking particularly at those grant-aided improvements, such as for certain types of insulation, which will cut your fuel bills in the future, and increase the price you will get for the property should you sell up later.

There are no longer any tax advantages to having a home or home improvement loan. The only exception to this is, as a concession to older people, anyone over 65 with a home income plan will continue to receive the tax relief, although no new home income plans will qualify.

You can now put an unlimited amount into your pension each year, subject to your total fund reaching a maximum of £1.5m. However, the maximum yearly investment which qualifies for tax relief is now the equivalent of once times your annual salary up to a maximum of £215,000.

Chapter four
YOUR STATE PENSION EXPLAINED

Working out what you are entitled to

PROVIDED you have paid enough National Insurance contributions then at the very least you will be entitled to the full basic State Pension paid at 65 to men and currently 60 to women. This age limit will be gradually equalised at 65 for both men and women, starting in 2010, but this won't affect women born before 6th april 1950.

To qualify for a full pension, you must have been making full contributions for at least nine-tenths of your working life, that is 39 years for women and 44 for men. However, in 2010 you will only need 30 years contributions although the credits for HRP (see below)from that date may not be applicable.

Every week you are at work, your employer makes contributions on your behalf. You may be credited for any you miss in certain circumstances – if you are unemployed, for instance or in full-time education or caring for a relative at home.

Even if you don't qualify for a full pension, you may well be entitled to a scaled-down one.

It's only if you have not managed to notch up contributions for at least ten years that you won't be eligible for any at all.

Most of those retiring in this position will be women who spent many years at home bringing up children or looking after dependants.

Since 1978, women in this situation have been able to claim Home Responsibilities Protection (HRP) which reduces the number of years required to make up a pension. However, as this protection is not allowed to be backdated it has come too late to help most of those retiring now.

If you have just been working overseas, you may have been credited with NICs. If you can't get details from your local DWP office, write to the DWP Overseas Pensions branch, Longbenton, Newcastle-upon-Tyne. NE98 1YX.

What you will get

SO HOW do you find out what you will get? You can do this quite easily now by contacting the DWP special Retirement Pensions Forecasting Advice Unit.

Just ask your local Social Security office for Form BR19 "Retirement Pension forecast", fill it in and send it off to the address in Newcastle listed on the form.

As well as the basic State Pension you can expect, the Forecasting Unit can also tell you of any additional pension you might be entitled to plus any Graduated Retirement Benefit based on the old graduated scheme which ran from 1961 to 1976.

Depending on what you paid then, you could get a few pounds extra each week on top of your basic State Pension.

You may also be entitled to extra pension from the scheme that replaced it, called SERPS, the State Earnings Related Pension Scheme. If you are in a pension scheme at work, you may be contracted out of this, in which case your employer must provide a pension at least equivalent to that which the State system would have paid out to you.

The forecasting unit will be able to tell you if you are eligible for any SERPS benefit.

Serps or state second pension

SERPS (State Earnings Related Pension Scheme) is an extra State pension which, as its name implies, bears some relation to your earnings, and is paid on top of the basic State pension.

Because there are so many permutations it is impossible to explain how much you can expect from SERPS. It is complicated by the fact that it is was replaced in April 2002 by the Second State Pension, and anyone who reaches pensionable age after April 1999 will get progressively less from it. Further, if your occupational pension scheme has 'contracted out' of SERPS, the Government won't pay your SERPS pension for those years.

But the proportion it would have paid will be included in your occupational scheme.

SERPS works like this: for every year since April 1978 that you have paid full NI contributions you will be credited with 1/80th of your total 'surplus earnings'.

State Earnings-Related Pension Scheme (SERPS)

You may have an employer who has 'contracted out' of SERPS. In this case, your NI contributions will be lower, but your State pension will not provide the 'additional' amount. Instead, your employer will have been deducting contributions for your occupational scheme, part of which will provide a 'guaranteed minimum pension' (GMP) at least as good as what you would have earned with SERPS.

If you have changed jobs, you may find you have an additional pension from SERPS and a guaranteed minimum pension, if different employers have chosen to contract in or out of SERPS. You will not get SERPs benefits for years in which you were self employed or chose to contract out of SERPs into a personal pension scheme.

Anyone who reaches state retirement age prior to 5th October 2002 will inherit all of their late spouse's SERPS, however, the Government is halving this entitlement.

The change will be phased in over a ten year period. See our chart for how it may affect you:

How The Phasing in will work:

		DATE
% of SERPS passing to surviving spouse when contributor reaches pension age.	100%	5.10.02 or earlier
	90%	6.10.02 – 5.10.04
	80%	6.10.04 – 5.10.06
	70%	6.10.06 – 5.10.08
	60%	6.10.08 – 5.10.10
	50%	6.10.10 or later

FORECASTING YOUR PENSION

THE key to finding this out is filling in the special form BR19 correctly. Phone and get them to send it to you if that's easier – if you don't know the number look in the phone book under "Social Security".

The secret is to give all the information asked for when you can, even if some of the questions seem a bit unnecessary. The form doesn't always explain the logic behind each question...

On the other hand don't worry if you can't answer them all – you might not be able to remember your National Insurance number, for instance. The DWP can usually trace this through your name and date of birth. Otherwise they may ask you to check with your last employer.

Alternatively they may start a search through their local office – but then officials need to know if you have ever changed your name. The form will ask you this and it pays to give all the surnames you have ever had including, in the case of a woman, her maiden name or former married name, if widowed or divorced.

The chief reason for this is the rule that allows any gaps in the National Insurance contribution record to be filled from the other partner's record where possible. This is allowed until the end of the tax year in which a divorce takes place.

It makes no difference to the other person, who probably won't even know.

Anyone expecting to get divorced within the current tax year gets two forecasts in fact – one on the assumption that they will still be married and the other assuming that the divorce has gone through.

What if a couple are separated? Well, until you actually get a divorce you are treated as still married for pension purposes.

CONTRIBUTION CREDITS

YOU will also be expected to answer questions about benefits you are claiming – you may then be entitled to some sort of credit for the contributions you aren't making, because you are currently claiming Jobseekers Allowance, for instance.

In this same section there are extra questions about Child Benefit. The person whose name appears above the address on the cover of the book is regarded as the "main payee".

This entitles them to the Home Responsibilities Protection mentioned earlier, in case looking after their children has meant a gap in their National Insurance contribution record because they haven't gone out to work. That way their State Pension is protected for that time.

You may also be entitled to credits if you have lived abroad. If there was some sort of reciprocal agreement with that particular country, your contribution record is more likely to be up to date.

European Community countries have these special arrangements, as do some Commonwealth ones.

WHICH RATE?

BUT whatever the forecast reveals there is a chance you could make up some of the missing contributions... or take advantage of some of the more recent changes to the way the contributions system now works.

Since October 1989, for example, women on low wages who elected to pay the special "married woman's stamp" when it was on offer – which ruled out a State Pension of their own – could find they would now get a better deal if they switched to paying the full contribution.

National Insurance contributions are earnings-related but what has changed is the way this is calculated and women earning less than, say, £60 a week could find they would actually be paying less on the full rate.

But it's worth remembering that once a woman makes the switch there is no going back, so before opting to "switch" in this way she would have to be sure it was the right thing and her wages were not suddenly going to increase dramatically, resulting in a larger National Insurance Contribution.

She would need to check out the switch carefully to see if there was still time for her to benefit with her own pension and this is where her official forecast should be able to help.

Pension Credit

From October 2003 the Minimum Income Guarantee (MIG) for pensioners was replaced by the pension credit, though the principal of a guaranteed minimum income continues to apply.

For people aged 60 and over the pension credit will guarantee an income of at least £124.05 a week for a single person and £189.35 for a married couple. This is the standard minimum guarantee. In MIG people are excluded from any help if they have savings of more than £12,000 (or £16,000 for care and nursing home residents). The pension credit abolishes this rule, and savings of £6,000 or less (£10,000 or less for nursing home residents) will be ignored.

In addition, single people over 65 and married couples where one is 65 may be entitled to a savings credit, aimed at rewarding people who have saved towards their own retirement with an additional 'top up'.

The savings credit will be based on income and calculated by taking into account any qualifying income above a fixed threshold – called the savings credit threshold. This threshold is £91.20 and £145.80 for couples. The maximum savings credit element is £19.71 a week for single people and £26.13 for couples.

Those on the lowest incomes will gain the most from the new

system. For example, someone with only £90 a week income will get a pension credit of £34.05, while someone with £110 a week will receive an extra £14.05 a week. Couples on £150 a week will get a pension credit of £39.35, while couples with £180 a week will qualify for a top-up of £9.35.

THE RATES WILL BE AS FOLLOWS:

Standard minimum guarantee
Single   £124.05
Couple   £189.35

Additional amount
for severe disability
Single   £50.55
Couple (where both qualify)   £100.70

Savings credit threshold
Single   £91.20
Couple   £145.80
Capital
Amount disregarded   £6,000
For anyone in a care home   £10,000

Deemed income £1 for each complete £500 or part thereof in excess of the above amounts.

MARRIED WOMEN

If you are a wife who has never paid NI, or only paid the married woman's rate (an option withdrawn in April 1977), you will not qualify for either the basic State pension or a State Earnings Related Pension (SERPS) in your own right, but if your husband qualifies for a full pension you will be entitled to an amount to bring your joint pension up to the full entitlement (See page 134). This used to be paid jointly as the married couple's pension.

If your husband dies first, then you will qualify for the widow's pension which is the same as the basic pension. As a married woman who opted to pay the married woman's rate, you can start to build up your own State pension rights by paying the full stamp in future in order to qualify for a pension in your own right. But is it worth it?

By paying the full stamp for a minimum of 10 years, provided that you earn more than a specified amount, you will qualify for a pension for each year that you pay it. Also, you may begin to qualify for the Second State Pension.

However, married woman who have paid full National Insurance Contributions throughout their working life will get a full state pension in their own right. This can make a big difference to married couples because both partners will get the full single person's rate. Woman may find it is worth their while to make back NI contributions if it means they can get a full state pension. However, you can only go back a maximum of six years.

From April 1978 a woman who stopped work to bring up children has her state pension protected for those years. The missing years should be automatically covered by the Government's Home Responsibility Protection (HRP) scheme, provided that the mother was getting Child Benefit for a child under 16.

HRP protection also applies to people who have had to stay off work to look after a relative regularly for at least 35 hours a week, who was receiving Attendance Allowance, or Disability Living Allowance care component at the higher or middle rate.

Other people whose basic pension is protected are those who have been off work, perhaps through redundancy or illness. If they have been signing on or submitting medical certificates, their pension should be unaffected for that period because they will have NI credits.

MAKING UP FOR LOST TIME

ANYONE who has had an interrupted working life could find it would be worth their while making up for any lost contributions by paying for those missing years now. You are only allowed this voluntary back-dating for lapses in the last six years – and you can only do this before retirement.

If you ask, officials can show you in your forecast what would happen if you decided to make up any "lost" contributions like this.

Worth noting – a woman who paid into this scheme can claim even if she's not entitled to a basic State Pension because of her contribution record. So, even if she's waiting for her husband to retire, she can still get something.

PENSIONS FROM JOBS

THE rules on the maximum pension you can receive have changed totally from April 2006. Before you could receive only two thirds of your final salary as a maximum. Now there is no maxium, but control is at the contribution end. Your total pension fund cannot exceed £1.65m in 2008/9.

You are restricted to the amount you may put into the fund each year – once times salary up to £235,000.

The majority of pension schemes are "contracted out" of the State Earnings Related Pension Scheme (SERPS). You get an ordinary basic State Pension based on your contribution record, but if your scheme has been contracted out then the extra pension you get comes from your employer rather than the State.

Most good employers will keep you informed by giving out annual statements about how your pension is building up. You have the right under the Disclosure of Information Regulations 1986 to insist that they do. There are strict time limits in which the adminstrator of Trustees must reply to your queries.

Details of your scheme's benefits are often in a booklet handed out to all members. The law actually says these booklets should be kept up to date, but that doesn't always happen in reality. If it's a while since yours was updated, it is worth double checking that nothing has changed. On the booklet there will be an address where you can write if you want more information.

There are several sorts of pension schemes, but most employer-run schemes are of the sort called "final earnings". With these the pension is worked out according to a set formula. But the exact definitions can make a big difference.

You might find your scheme gives a pension based on all your earnings in the last year before you retire. Others take account only of basic earnings, without making any allowance for overtime or commission. What's regarded as "pensionable service" also varies from one occupational pension scheme to another.

Sometimes you have to put in a couple of years' work before you are allowed to join and, depending on the rules of your employer's scheme, this time may or may not count in the final calculations.

With some schemes, you may be given the opportunity to "buy" the extra years.

That's why it would pay you to go through the small print of your booklet to see exactly what you're going to get (and what your spouse would receive on your death) – and there's nothing to stop you trying to get the scheme improved. There may be a special committee you can approach, or your trade union may help.

INFLATION-PROOFING

BEFORE retiring, check how much pension your company will pay you and how far it is inflation-proof. Employees in the public sector like the Civil Service, local authorities, NHS and teachers will get inflation-proofed pensions automatically. But employees in the private sector may get little inflation-proofing built in.

Since January 1st 1991, if an employee leaves a Company pension scheme early, and doesn't take an immediate pension, the *eventual* pension must be re-valued at 5%, or the retail price index which ever is lower. Company pensions in payment must also be uprated in line with prices up to 5% (though this indexation only applies to pension rights earned after April 6 1997).

If you have changed jobs you may have left some pension rights behind with a former employer and may have lost track of them. If so, the Registry of Pension Schemes may be able to help. The address is PO Box 1NN, Newcastle upon Tyne, NE99 1NN. Tel: 0191 225 6316, website: www.opra.gov.uk.

If any former employer has moved or gone out of business, the pension fund should still be in operation, as the trustees have a duty to administer the scheme while there are still beneficiaries.

LUMP SUM PAYMENTS

SOMETIMES it is possible to give up part of your pension in

return for a one-off lump sum payment. In official jargon, this is called "commuting" your pension. As a rough guide, a man aged 65 could get a cash sum of £900 for every £100 a year of pension he gives up, whereas a woman of 60 might get £1,100 for every £100 a year of pension she gives up. The difference is because statistically she is expected to draw her pension for longer.

But this difference doesn't always apply, it depends on the particular scheme. The most you can have in a lump sum 25% of your total pension fund, but most people get a lot less.

Many people find the option of commuting attractive, as it gives them a lump sum to invest as comforting nest-egg for the future or spend on something specific – like a once-in-a-lifetime holiday.

Only you can decide whether commuting is a good idea, depending on personal circumstances, your health and dependants.

If you have to retire early because of ill health, you are unlikely to be penalised – in fact some schemes are boosted for the sick.

Otherwise going early is likely to cost you as, understandably, the longer you are likely to receive a pension, the more the money you put in has to be stretched. Also, you will have paid in less than someone working to retirement age.

AVCS

Employers must allow staff to pay AVCs to a maximum one times salary up to £215,000 per year less all other pensions contributions.

However, as no contributions are paid by your employer, the investment does not grow in the same way as your main occupational pension.

You are now able to commute part of your AVCs to give a lump sum, but a smaller pension

STAKEHOLDER PENSIONS

Stakeholder Pensions were introduced in April 2001, with strict rules to make them cheap and simple. They're primarily aimed at the lower paid, the young and those that have no access to an occupational pension scheme, but they nevertheless have a relevance to older people.

For the first time ever you can pay into a pension scheme out of unearned income and you can pay in on behalf of someone else. The pension fund will get the full tax relief on the contributions, so in order to achieve the maximum allowable contribution of £3,600 a year you need only actually part with £2,808. Husbands can now pay into pensions schemes for non-working wives, grandparents and parents can contribute on behalf of children and young adults.

Stakeholder pensions are also an alternative to AVCs for older emplyees, and may be better in that you can take a 25% tax-free lump sum on retirement, whereas with AVCs the whole amount must be used to buy a pension. With a Stakeholder pension you can also take benefits from age 50 to 75 and there is no need to retire first.

How to complain

THE Pensions Ombudsman deals with individual complaints. He works in conjunction with the Occupational Pensions Advisory Service, a voluntary outfit which offers advice to individuals. Contact OPAS at 11 Belgrave Road, London, SW1V 1RB. Tel: 0845 6012923 (local call rate helpline). Email: enquiries@opas.org.uk, website: www.opas.org.uk.

Chapter five

STATE BENEFITS AND YOUR RIGHTS

A guide to your entitlements

IT'S A sad fact that many pensioners do find it extra hard to make ends meet, but there are benefits they could be entitled to which can help.

The most important point to remember is that they have been paid for through National Insurance contributions over the years – and the benefits are the right of those entitled to them. This is not charity and it's essential to know just what is available and who can claim it.

INCOME SUPPORT

THIS replaced the old Supplementary Benefit. To qualify your savings must be £16,000 or less (If you or your partner are aged over 60 Pension Credit may apply) and neither you nor your partner should work for 16 hours a week or more.

To calculate whether or not you are then entitled to the benefit you must first add up all your savings, apart from the value of your home, and the surrender value of your life insurance policy.

If these total more than £6,000, the benefit will be gradually scaled down by £1 per £250 of savings to a cut-off limit of £16,000 when Income Support ceases. Next you must list your weekly income – that's all the money coming to you after tax and National Insurance have been paid. For these calculations you don't need to include some other benefits you might be claiming such as Housing Benefit, Disability Living or Attendance Allowance or income from savings below the £16,000 limit.

But you would need to check all this out very carefully with the DWP – it is complicated. For instance, if you let out a room in your house, how much of the rent you can discount depends on whether heating costs are included in the rent or not.

What money you actually get depends on the sum the DWP calculates you need to live on each week. If you have less than this sum, you can claim Income Support to make up the difference.

All this is explained in booklet IS1, A Guide to Income Support, from the DWP – if you need help filling the claim form in, your Citizens Advice Bureau (address in the phone book) or Welfare Rights Agency are a good bet. As a rule, this benefit would be added to your retirement pension and paid out with it.

SOCIAL FUND

WHAT this does is provide cash for a variety of one-off payments from cold weather help to funeral costs. Someone responsible for the costs of a funeral who is already on Income Support, Housing Benefit, or Council Tax Benefit would be eligible to apply for funeral grants.

Savings no longer have any effect on suitability for funeral payments. Now the sole criteria is whether you are in receipt of one the benefits mentioned.

Pensioners claiming Income Support or Pension Credit may be entitled to extra help to meet the costs of fuel during very cold weather through this particular fund. A payment of £8.50 will automatically be made for any seven-day period when the average temperature is 0°C or below.

COMMUNITY CARE GRANT

THESE grants do not have to be repaid. They are available to people on Income Support, including elderly people with restricted mobility as well as the disabled.

You can get a grant to help with moving from institutional or residential care back into the community to cover such things as bedding, cookers, fuel connections, removal charges and so on.

Discretionary Community Care Grants are also available to help someone avoid going into care by paying for "essentials" like furniture and minor household repairs and for families under pressure facing disability, chronic sickness or breakdown of marriage.

Finally, you can get a Community Care Grant to help with urgent and often unexpected travel expenses, such as visiting someone in hospital or attending a close relative's funeral. Each DWP office has a strict budget limit, and grants can be hard to get.

WHEN IT'S ONLY A LOAN'S

THE other payments made through the Social Fund are only loans. Again, they are only granted at the Social Fund Officer's discretion and must normally be repaid within 18 months. Normally this is done by deducting what you owe from your other regular benefit payments. Though the loans are discretionary, the Social Fund Officer works within a legal framework and according to a defined set of rules, but to a strictly limited budget for his area.

Once this budget has been used up there is literally no more money available for applicants to the fund. This is the main reason why the loans are not yours by right.

There are basically two types of loan, so you need to be clear which type you are entitled to and which covers your needs.

The first are BUDGET LOANS which are restricted to those who have been on Income Support for at least 26 weeks and need essential items they could not otherwise afford.

The Social Fund Officer is expected to give priority to applications for such basics as bedding, clothing and moving costs and not "luxury" items like a TV set, for example. But in poorer areas where the demands on the Fund are greatest, the cash limits mean you may be refused a loan even for something deemed an essential item.

The loan will be deducted at a rate of between 5% and 15% from your Income Support, for up to 18 months. It's important to take into account the cost of repayment. The loans are interest-free but repayments will still make a hole in your Income Support.

CRISIS LOANS are different because they are not restricted to people on Income Support. As their name suggests, they are for emergencies such as fire or flood or if the cooker breaks down, and other situations where your health or safety have been put at serious risk. Again, they are only granted at the discretion of the Social Fund Office, which will take into account your savings and income, the size of the loan and the period over which you must repay it. But most important, the office will also check out whether the cash help is available from any other sources – local government for example, or charity.

How to claim

YOU apply for either a loan or a grant on claim form SF300 available from your local DWP office. Try to include as much additional information as possible, even if you put it on an extra sheet of paper. Obviously, the grant offers a much better deal than a loan which is why it can be worth enlisting some expert help with filling in the form. Try your Citizens Advice Bureau (address in the phone book) which will have people used to dealing with these forms.

If you are turned down then your right of appeal is limited and the final decision rests with the Department of Social Security whose officer refused you the money in the first place.

Housing benefit

THIS is an important benefit for those on low incomes – it's basically non-taxable help with rent for those on a very tight budget.

Housing Benefit, also called rent rebate or rent allowance, is administered by the local authority under rules drafted by the Government.

WORKING IT OUT

IF THE kind of accommodation you have is specially geared up for the elderly and the rent includes service charges for such things as cleaning, portering, caretaking and rubbish removal and the cost of the emergency alarm system, then the maximum benefit you could claim is 100%.

To see if you may be eligible, the first step is to calculate your weekly rent. If you have other people sharing your home with you, you can deduct a certain amount from these figures for people other than your partner aged 18 and over who live in your home. How much you deduct depends on the age and circumstances of the person concerned.

The next step is to add up the value of your savings, including cash, bank, building society and National Savings Accounts, National Savings Certificates, Premium Bonds, stocks and shares and half of any joint savings you may have with someone else. For a couple you take both your savings but the following exclusion limits remain the same for both couples and single people: savings of £3,000 or less are discounted but between £3,000 and £16,000 will affect the benefit.

You must then add up your weekly income to a set formula – you are allowed to ignore some benefits, for instance. And if it is the same or less than the Government figure for what you need you may well be entitled to have help with your rent.

COUNCIL TAX

Council Tax, came into force in April 1993. It takes into account the value of your property within eight bands and the number of people living there.

People with no more than £16,000 in savings and on a low income may be entitled to 100% Council Tax Benefit. If you are claiming Housing Benefit then it's likely the council has sent you a claim form for Council Tax Benefit.

The householder is responsible for the payment. Joint owners, such as husband and wife, are jointly responsible. A discount of

25% is given when only one person lives in the property. When the property is empty, the owner gets a 50% discount. Other discounts are available to people with disabilities, and people who are carers.

If you don't agree with the council's assessment, you have the right to appeal. First you can ask officials to take another look at their calculations, but if you still aren't satisfied then you can ask to have the decision reviewed by a local review board.

Age Concern publishes a free information sheet called The Council Tax and Older People, available on receipt of a large SAE, from Age Concern England, 1268 London Road, London, SW16 4ER.

INCAPACITY BENEFIT

April 1995, Incapacity Benefit replaced Invalidity Benefit and Sickness Benefit.

Incapacity Benefit is paid to people who are assessed as being incapable of working, so long as they have paid sufficient National Insurance contributions to qualify for this benefit.

Incapacity Benefit is paid at three basic rates: a short-term lower rate for those unable to work for up to 28 weeks; a short-term higher rate paid between 29 and 52 weeks; and a long-term rate paid after a year. (Statutory Sick Pay continues to be paid for the first 28 weeks of sickness for most people who work for an employer.)

The short-term higher rate and long-term rate of Incapacity Benefit are taxable. Long-term Incapacity Benefit stops once you reach State pensioner age and claim your pension.

In addition to the basic rate of Incapacity Benefit, there are other supplements, such as Adult Dependency Increase, Child Dependency Increase, and Age Addition.

The rules are different if you were receiving Invalidity Benefit before the new benefit was introduced. In this case you will be paid under the old Invalidity Benefit rules and your benefit will not be taxable.

For more details, ask your Social Security office for the Incapacity Benefit leaflet (IB202).

SEVERE DISABLEMENT ALLOWANCE

One tax-free benefit which must be claimed before you reach State pension age is Severe Disablement Allowance (SDA).

This is paid to people who cannot work because of illness or disablement but who do not qualify for other benefits, such as Incapacity Benefit, because they have not paid enough NI contributions.

You must have been unable to work for at least 28 weeks and be below pension age when you apply for this allowance, as well as having been resident in the UK for 10 out of the previous 20 years.

Your particular disability will be assessed on a percentage scale according to a rather complicated set of rules. Unless you were disabled before the age of 21, you must be what's officially termed 80% disabled or getting other benefits such as Disability Living or Attendance Allowance.

DISABILITY LIVING ALLOWANCE (DLA)
MOBILITY COMPONENT

THE Mobility Component of the Disability Living Allowance can only be claimed by someone under 66. It is for people who have a problem moving about or need someone with them when they go outside. There are two rates – higher rate and lower rate, depending on how much help you need.

It does not depend on National Insurance contributions, nor is it subject to any savings or earnings limits and it is not taxable .

The other important point is that drawing it does not affect your other pension or bencfits. In other words, once you meet the qualifying conditions, this is yours by right and nothing else you claim is affected.

You qualify if you have become fully or virtually unable to walk through a physical disability before the age of 65 (for both men and women in this case).

This problem must be likely to remain for at least a year. You must also have been living in the UK for a year out of the previous 18 months.

The claim must be in at the latest by your 66th birthday. Claimants get some other incorporated benefits too. Someone on the higher rate of the Mobility Component of the DLA who is still able to drive a car in some form does not need to pay any Road Tax. If someone else uses a car mostly to meet their needs – a son or daughter perhaps – then they, too, can claim Road Tax Exemption.

Claimants can also apply to the local council to join the Blue Badge Scheme for which there is sometimes a small charge, but this varies from area to area. This allows free parking in certain restricted areas. This concession is also available to another driver using the car mainly on their behalf.

To claim Mobility Component of the DLA, contact your local DWP office for a form, from which they will base their decision whether to grant it. (See page 135)

DLA – CARE COMPONENT

THIS is available for anyone under 65. There are three rates according to how much care you need. The highest is for day and night-time care; the middle rate and lower rate is aimed at people whose disability is less severe.

Since there have been several well publicised and controversial cases where these allowances have been refused, seek expert advice from your Citizens Advice Bureau in the event of any appeal.

(See page 135)

CARER'S ALLOWANCE

THIS allowance is not made to the disabled person himself but to those under pensionable age who are unable to work because they are caring for a disabled person. The disabled person they are looking after does not necessarily have to be a relative or even live in the same house. The allowance is currently £50.55.

There is an additional allowance for a dependant adult and another for a dependant child.

This benefit does not depend on National Insurance contributions, but the person being cared for must be getting Attendance Allowance or Disability Living Allowance at middle or higher rates. The person doing the caring must do so for at least 35 hours a week and therefore be unavailable for work.

There are other conditions, too. While the carer can be married or single, he or she must be over 16 and under pensionable age, a UK resident and have lived here for at least 26 weeks in the past year. In addition, extra earnings are restricted, though "reasonable expenses" are permitted.

The DWP goes to great lengths to make sure this particular benefit is not abused and claimants already in receipt of some other Social Security benefits are disbarred from it. While you draw Carer's Allowance, your National Insurance contributions are automatically credited to safeguard your future pension rights.

Attendance allowance

ATTENDANCE Allowance – which is not taxable and is usually paid with the State Pension – is meant for those disabled people, aged 65 and over, who need attention and special supervision.

The rules allow for as wide a range of people as possible to draw it, but the person must have been resident in the UK and have been here for at least 26 weeks in the past year. They must also have needed the "attention" of another person for at least six months.

That person might be a nurse or relative and does not have to live in, so the Allowance is even payable to those who live on their own and whose helpers visit.

You may find yourself looking after an elderly relative who qualifies for Attendance Allowance. If so, help them claim it.

There are two rates paid weekly, a higher rate and a lower rate.

The disability can be either physical or mental. Which rate the person is entitled to will depend on how much attention the disability requires and how many of the ordinary functions the person can perform. To get the lower rate, the person must fulfil either day-time or night-time conditions, for the higher Attendance Allowance they must fulfil both.

The day-time conditions require that the person claiming needs frequent attention to cope with normal bodily functions such as eating, going to the toilet or simply moving about. The Allowance is also available on the grounds that he or she needs supervision to avoid putting themselves or others in danger.

The night-time conditions are similar but "prolonged or repeated attention" must be needed during the night for periods of up to 30 minutes or at least twice. As a rough guide, those claiming the night-time allowance are generally more disabled. Someone who needs a carer to watch over them all through the night is also eligible.

As the Allowance is dependent on a person's medical condition it won't be paid instantly. To qualify, a person must have been suffering the condition for six months, though a claim can be put in after three months.

If someone claiming the Allowance has to go into hospital where supervision is available round the clock, or has to go into a local authority home, for instance, the Allowance is stopped after 28 days.

Someone already in hospital or a council home can't claim the allowance, of course, except for days out. Should they be paying the full cost of private treatment or care then it will still be paid. If they travel abroad – for medical treatment perhaps – then they should still be able to get Attendance Allowance.

The Attendance Allowance is claimed through the local DWP office on a self-assessment form. You will be asked for details of what you find particularly difficult to do and why. It's not just the physical things that will help win the Allowance, but the side-effects like tiredness and lack of concentration, for instance.

You will not normally have to undergo a medical examination.

Not every applicant is successful the first time round. If this happens it is worth asking for a review of your case – statistics show that over half the review cases are eventually successful. (See page 135)

COMMUNITY CARE

While local authorities are under an obligation to provide adequate facilities, in some areas, there is not enough money to pay for it. So provision for the elderly will vary from county to county. Depending on the policies and budgets of each local authority, this could mean increased fees, fewer residential and nursing home places, and fewer independent inspectors to monitor premises and conditions. This may put a greater strain on you if you are looking after a sick or elderly relative.

Once you are referred to social services for long term care, you will be means tested to see whether you should pay some or all, accommodation and personal care costs (unless you live in Scotland). Only medical care via a registered nurse is free to everyone. If you live in Scotland you pay accommodtion charges only. Age Concern Scotland (0800 009 966) for leaflets and information.

Before anyone is entitled to care provision, they are assessed, firstly on need, and secondly on financial status.

The local authority assesses how much you should pay based on your income and savings. If you have £16,000 or more in savings, you will not qualify for help until your savings fall below this figure.

Your local authority even has the right to stake a claim against the value of your property, from the day you go into a home, to cover the cost of the care element.

If your partner still lives in your joint property, don't worry – the place won't be sold under them! If your house is occupied by a relative who is incapacitated, or aged over 60, the value of the property won't be taken into account when the authorities assess your liability to pay your nursing or residential home fees.

As an alternative to providing care places, many local authorities in Britain encourage "Care in the Community", a euphemism for relatives, friends and neighbours looking after people who remain in their own home but who are no longer able to cope by themselves.

If you find yourself in the position of needing help (or of looking after a frail or elderly relative), first ask what support services your local authority provides, such as domiciliary care workers. Then find out whether you are eligible for Attendance Allowance at either the lower or higher rate.

Invalid Care Allowance can be claimed by anyone below State pension age who can't work full-time because they look after a severely disabled person for at least 35 hours a week. Ring the DWP Benefits Enquiry Freephone on 0800 882200 for details.

Bereavement Benefits

Since April 9th 2001 both men and women not receiving a state pension will receive a lump sum payment of £2,000, a bereavement allowance if they are over 45, but only for 52 weeks, and anyone with children in full-time education will get a widowed parent's allowance. Once a widow is 60 she may be entitled to a State Retirement Pension in her own right based on her husband's record.

The Retirement Pension for Widows, which is also taxable, can be claimed by women who were over 60 when their husband died and is based on his contributions. The maximum she can receive is the single person's retirement pension. Once she is retired, a woman can keep this pension if she remarries or moves in with someone.

Making an Appeal

ADJUDICATION Officers decide on claims for Social Security benefits and anyone who disagrees with such a decision can complain to the Social Security Appeal Tribunal, which is a legally qualified body independent of the DWP.

The first step is to write to your local DWP office within three months of being turned down for something, including full details of your case. It's a good idea to enlist the help of your Citizens Advice Bureau.

Sometimes the decision may be reversed there and then under this review procedure. Otherwise it goes to tribunal.

Details of your case and a time and date for the hearing will be sent to you. Proceedings are always informal and you will receive travelling expenses. You are unlikely to be told the results then and there. The three panel members can only change the original decision if the regulations have been breached in some way, not just if the treatment seems a bit unfair; they cannot pay more money than the law allows.

More information

IF YOU want to know more about Social Security Benefits and National Insurance ask your local DWP Benefits Agency office for advice, or use the website; www.dwp.gov.uk/lifeevents/benefits

There is a special Benefit Enquiry Line for people with disabilities on Freephone 0800 882200.

See the Social Security benefits table on page 134 for the main National Insurance Benefits you can claim.

These Social Security leaflets are some of the many available free from your local DWP office:

RM1	Retirement
RM2	Approaching retirement?
RM3	Retired?
SD1	Sick or Disabled
SD3	Long-term ill or disabled?
SD4	Caring for someone?
SD5	Ill or disabled because of work?
GL14	Widowed?
GL18	Needing help from the Social Fund?
GL23	Benefit rates
RR2	A guide to housing benefit and council tax benefit
IS 20	Income Support
DS 702	Attendance Allowance

DS 704	Disability Living Allowance
CWP1	Cold Weather Payment
NP46	A Guide to Retirement Pensions
CA 01	National Insurance for Employees
FC1	Family Credit (for working families)
N1 246	How to appeal
IB202	Incapacity Benefit
NP45	Widows' benefits
CA 07	Unpaid and late paid contributions
NI 38	Social Security abroad
Are you entitled to help with health costs?	
AP 1	Helping Hand (disability)
HB6	Equipment and Services for Disabled People
SB 16	Guide to the Social Fund
NI 2	If you have an industrial disease
JSA L5	Jobseeker's Allowance

Special benefit enquiry line for people with disabilities:
Freephone 0800 882 200
State Pensions help on website: www.thepensionsservice.gov.uk or check at local benefit office for local customer service number.
War Pensions Helpline: 01253 858 858. Ask for leaflet WPA 1: Notes about War Disablement Pension and War Widows' Pensions.

Chapter six
YOUR PERKS

*Take advantage of all
the concessions available*

THE good news is that there are a host of bargains waiting for you the minute you become an "official" pensioner. Some of them depend on where you live – some local authorities are far more generous than others.

CHEAPER TRAVEL

THE UK rail network has some particularly good offers – what's more some of them start before retirement. Anyone over 60, for instance, can apply for a Senior Citizen's Railcard entitling them to half-price, cheap day return fares. In addition you get a third off standard singles and returns, saver returns, some network breaks, 1st class single and return plus Rail Rovers.

For those still commuting to work, one of these cards can offer a better deal than some season tickets, certainly if you are not going in every day of the week and this is something well worth investigating. This is particularly true if you can travel off-peak.

If you are going by train to Europe some cross-Channel ferry companies will also grant a discount of up to a third when such voyages are part of a rail/sea journey. There are similar discounts available on some long distance British bus and coach routes, too. You may find some airlines also offer concessionary fares for pensioners.

Bus passes should be available offering free off peak travel within your area. You may be able to "bus hop" from place to place providing you use service buses not national coaches.

In the meantime, what's offered is usually down to individual local authorities, it does vary considerably. You may find that residents in the next street to you get free travel because it comes under a different authority to yours where there are, perhaps, no concessions at all. This is obviously a consideration, as is the quality of bus services in deciding where to spend your retirement.

But bus passes apart, as a rule it pays to check out just what reduction you can claim whenever you take a trip anywhere. Compare the costs and check out what's offered to pensioners. Going midweek, for instance, could sometimes halve what you have to pay.

There are reductions on certain holidays too, as well as some specially geared up for pensioners. You can get in virtually anywhere – from museums to art galleries – at a reduced rate or free of charge.

INSURANCE INCENTIVES

AN INCREASING number of special insurance deals are coming on to the market for the over 50s, offering a variety of benefits like reduced premiums and extra services.

Motor insurance is one example – Mature drivers are considered a "good risk", having fewer accidents than younger drivers, up until the age of 70. However, once you are over 70, you may find your premiums rocket, and you should look then, if not before, at insurance companies which specialise in mature drivers (generally defined as over 50), who won't penalise you for your age. If you have been with the same company for number of years, and have have built up a no-claims bonus, you should be able to transfer this to a new company.

House insurance is another important area where your age could be of positive benefit. For although your age doesn't affect your chances of being burgled, statistics show that older people are at home more and are more security-conscious. Insurers, recognising this, have a number of schemes that can reduce your annual premium.

Remember, too, that a number of insurance companies offer cheaper premiums if you can prove you belong to a Neighbourhood Watch scheme, if you have fitted good quality security locks and approved alarms.

Private medical insurance is another highly competitive area but bear in mind tax relief on premiums relating to the over 60s has been abolished.

Holiday and travel insurance is something you may need to consider, especially if you are hoping to go away more often now you have more leisure time. An annual multi-trip policy may work out cheaper than single-trip insurance, and again there are companies specialising in older customers. Premiums tend to go up for the over 65s, but you can avoid the higher charges by shopping around.

Looking good

VIRTUALLY all hairdressing salons offer some "specials" for pensioners. Sometimes there's a special day when you can get a hairdo for about half price. The same applies to beauty salons – you may find manicures, facials and massage are all reduced for pensioners on a particular day.

Your local authority may run exercise classes with a reduced rate for pensioners – or even a special Keep Fit class specifically for them. Ask your Social Services Department at the Town Hall if they know about local concessions for pensioners. Many now keep a useful list which includes not just the things they run themselves, but some others from elsewhere.

Entertainment is one area where there are always concesssions. Most cinemas, for instance, will let you in cheap for certain performances as will theatres – though normally only for matinees.

Bargains galore

MANY shops have discounts for pensioners... dry cleaners and shoe menders, for instance, may have special days when pensioners can get cut-price care.

Incidentally, if the libraries in your area still have a fines system for late books, this may well not apply to pensioners who can keep books out for as long as they like.

Prescriptions are free for anyone over 60 now (men included, thanks to EC ruling) – this can represent a big saving.

If you are under State retirement age and use many prescriptions, you can pay £27.85 a quarter (or £102.50 a year) for all your prescriptions, if this would work out more cheaply for you. Tel: 0845 850 0030.

And at Christmas there is a £10 bonus paid to anyone receiving State Pension. You get this at the beginning of December every year. It should come automatically.

Chapter seven
TAX WHEN YOU'RE RETIRED

Your responsibilities explained

While at work most of our income is from wages or salary from which PAYE tax has been already taken, so we receive it 'net'. When we retire the same will apply to any occupational pension we receive from our employer.

In retirement some of your income will come from the State pension, which is part of your taxable income. No tax is taken out before you receive it, but if your total income exceeds your personal tax allowance you will have to pay tax on all, or part of, your State pension.

This tax will either be collected from you in one amount at the end of the tax year (so don't forget to allow for it), or from your occupational pension through an adjustment to your tax coding.

Also, in retirement part of our total income may be produced from investments. It is vital to understand that whether or not we pay tax, or how much tax we pay, will be determined by our choice of investment.

So do take into account the separate income tax and Capital Gains Tax allowances belonging to both husband and wife.

It is worth checking your income and tax deductions at the end of the tax year each April, to make sure that you have benefited fully from your tax allowances.

The Inland Revenue's leaflets IR121, IR90 and IR80 should help you identify if you have made full use of your allowances, and how to claim overpaid tax. Your local Tax Enquiry Centre will also help.

It's not really that daunting. The secret is to understand how the system works... and to plan ahead, starting with retirement itself.

If you're taking redundancy, for instance, and are one of the lucky few entitled to more than the maximum tax-free sum of £30,000, it would pay you to leave your company the other side of a new tax year.

Any allowances not used up on other parts of your income – and remember you're likely to be earning less when you retire – can then be used to cover for the money you get over the tax-free £30,000.

The opposite applies if all your pay-off comes into the tax-free category. Then it is most effective to take it in a high-earning year.

Personal allowances 2008/2009

A husband and wife are now each responsible for their own tax. And most important, each are able to claim their individual tax-free allowances.

These days everyone has a Personal Allowance £5,435 in the 2008/2009 tax year.

In the age group 65-74, the Personal Allowance for the tax year 2008/2009 is £9,030, for age 75-plus it's £9,180. But there is an income limit on this of £21,800.

Once it goes over the limit, it is scaled down by £1 for every £2 of income above the limit, until it reaches the basic allowances.

Married Couple's Allowance

Married Couple's Tax Allowance (MCA) was abolished from 5 April 2000, except where at least one partner was over the age of 65 on that date. Any single person over the age of 65 on 5 April who subsequently gets married will be entitled to MCA, but younger married people **do not** become entitled to it on their 65th birthday.

For couples old enough to continue receiving MCA, both this and the extra age allowances to which you are entitled after the age 65 (see page 130 for rates) qualify for tax relief at 10 per cent. Since April 1990 women over 65 qualify for age-related allowances in their own right. A married woman may now claim half the minimum Married Couple's Allowance to be set against her income.

Previously, the Married Couple's Allowance automatically went to the husband, unless his income was too low to make use of it.

Now a wife does not need her husband's permission to opt for the change. She simply informs the Inland Revenue on form 18 BEFORE the beginning of the tax year, and they will make the necessary change. She can then earn extra money before tax – but her husband will lose out by the same amount!

If both husband and wife are in the same tax bracket, there will be no change to the overall household income if the wife opts for her half share of the allowance. However, if a wife is in a higher tax bracket than her husband, she may be better off claiming her half of the Married Couple's Allowance. A husband can elect to transfer his half of his allowance to her as well. Once you have opted for change, the Inland Revenue will abide by your new arrangement until you inform them otherwise.

Of course, most partners in the same tax bracket would see no difference in their overall income. But the new rules can benefit couples where the wife earns more than the husband.

To prove the Independent Taxation revolution has finally come of age, a wife can claim not only her half of the Married Couple's Allowance, but all of it, with her husband's agreement. But where a husband is a 40% payer, with a wife paying at 22% or less, the couple would be worse off if the wife claimed her half.

The Inland Revenue will only consider half, all, or none of the Allowance to be transferred – not any other proportions. If they are not notified, they will continue to set the Married Couple's Allowance against the husband's income.

Once a wife stakes her claim, she will be allowed it each year until she notifies her tax office otherwise.

UNDERSTANDING 'INCOME'

NOT all the money you get is regarded as income as far as the Inland Revenue is concerned. But it's important to understand just what does come into this category... and what does not.

THIS IS INCOME:
* Pensions including what you get from the State.
* Earnings from any kind of work you do, including fees you may charge for a part-time job.
* Investment income, dividends, and the interest you get on savings where the tax hasn't already been deducted. This applies if you have money in any unit trusts, for instance, or a bank deposit account.
* Profits from a business.
* All earnings from being self-employed after allowable expenses.
* Many Social Security Benefits and any payments under Training and Enterprise Schemes for setting up a business.
* Any regular payments you get from elsewhere.

BUT THESE ARE TAX-FREE:
* Presents and gifts.
* Some money you inherit. Any Inheritance Tax owed will have already been paid, but Income Tax may be due if interest or

dividends were received by the executor before the money was passed to you.
* Rent from letting out a room in your house to a maximum £81.73 a week (£4,250 a year).
* Winnings from gambling, unless this is your business.
* Premium bond prizes, pools and lottery wins.
* Money from certain investments, such as TESSAs, PEPs and ISAs.
* Some Social Security benefits – Severe Disablement Allowance, Attendance Allowance, Mobility Component of the Disability Living Allowance, for instance, and Income Support if it's paid for reasons other than unemployment.
* Special grants – for insulating your home, for example.

TAX TIMING

THE tax year runs from April 6 to the following April 5. On income you receive between these two dates you pay tax once you breach the threshold of your personal allowances. People over 65 get a higher allowance. It is raised again at 75.

At the end of this book, we give you current tax tables and full details of the personal allowances for this tax year (2007/2008).

But basically the following are the allowances you can claim:

THE PERSONAL ALLOWANCE: Everyone under the age of 65 has a tax free Personal Allowance regardless of sex or marital status. The special Age Allowance means this will be worth more once you (or your spouse) reaches 65 – and even more at 75.

A wife who is not at work and therefore doesn't earn a salary can use her Allowance against any investment income she may have.

THE MARRIED COUPLE'S ALLOWANCE: On top of a personal allowance, a married couple also get this extra allowance, provided one partner was 65 before 5 April 2000.

Usually it will be set against the husband's income so that he will pay less tax unless the wife claims half of it.

SPECIAL ALLOWANCES: If you become eligible for the Age Allowance during a tax year you should get it automatically. But sometimes this can be overlooked. If you don't get it then contact your local tax office – address in the local phone book.

The normal Age Allowance for the over-65s can be backdated for up to six years, which could obviously give those eligible a handsome rebate.

Another allowance that can be set against income is the Blind Person's Allowance, which is available to registered blind people as individuals, a blind couple can each add to their allowance, less any tax-free disability payment received.

Of course, it's important to remember that these are allowances against tax – not grants – so there's no direct cash involved.

Relief v allowances

ON TOP of the tax allowances you can claim relief on certain expenditure, such as special charity covenants, pension contributions and so on.

Relief on private medical insurance was abolished in the July 1997 budget, though there are now some special budget schemes designed for the over-65s.

If you still have a way to go before retirement, you can sometimes also get additional tax relief through profit-related pay schemes at work, though these are being phased out.

Other tax savers

If you are still working there are tax advantages to be had from contributions you make to occupational pension schemes, any additional voluntary contributions the scheme allows along with relief on contributions to the personal pension schemes favoured by the self-employed. For approved schemes there is an earnings ceiling on which you can get this relief, as well as a maximum tax-free sum you can take when you retire.

With personal pension schemes, those aged 51 to 55 can claim tax relief of up to 30% of their annual salary, 35% if you are 56 or over, and 40% if you are 60 or over. There is also an earnings "cap" for pension contributions to new schemes of £215,000.

As far as investments are concerned, as a result of the 1995 Autumn Budget, tax on savings income is now charged at 20% if you are a basic rate tax payer. So any interest from building society or bank accounts will be paid net of 20% tax.

All about thresholds

OF COURSE there are some people, particularly retired people and wives not at work, whose "income" once they have claimed everything allowed is not high enough to make them liable to pay any tax at all.

Composite Rate Tax on bank and building society interest was scrapped in April 1991, so non-taxpayers can now claim back any tax they have over-paid on this type of savings scheme.

It's worth remembering that investments which pay "gross" – in other words before any tax has been deducted – can be a better bet.

If you are ever in any doubt about which of your investments have had tax already deducted then ask. You should declare them anyway. You can't be taxed twice and the banks and other institutions will have told the Inland Revenue of any substantial pay-outs they have made to you.

But what if the Inland Revenue does make a mistake? You will get the money back... eventually.

The secret is to keep putting the pressure on until the money is returned. However, you may have to wait till the next tax year.

Errors made in your favour are different. If you are charged too little tax and then the Inland Revenue discovers the error later you will get a demand for the outstanding amount.

If it's for a lot of money or you consider it unreasonable then you can use what's known as the Official Error procedure to get the matter fully investigated. This won't always work in your favour but when it does, you will usually only have to pay part of the bill and, occasionally, none of it at all.

Capital gains

IF YOU have your own business, or lots of "assets" like a second home, shares or antiques, then it won't just be Income Tax that interests you... there is also Capital Gains Tax to consider.

Tax-free

THERE are some things you can sell and not have to pay any Capital Gains Tax. Your home is probably your biggest asset but you don't have to pay CGT on any profit you make if you sell it as long as it is your only or your main residence.

If you have two homes then you can decide which one is your "principal private residence," to use official tax jargon.

You can sometimes be caught out if you sub-divide a large house into flats which you rent out or even if you simply use part of your home as an office and claim ordinary tax relief on it.

Any areas in your home deemed a business enterprise could then expose you to a capital gains penalty when you sell. In this situation you need to get professional accountancy advice – if you don't have an accountant then ask friends and family for recommendations.

Selling up

IF YOU own at least 5% of the shares in a business or a family company, then if you part with either you have to pay CGT. But if you wait until you are at least 50 when you take this step, or retiring through ill health, you could be eligible for Retirement Relief.

To qualify, you must be selling up to retire and, provided you have been working there full-time as a director and have owned the business or shares for at least one year, you could escape CGT.

Relief increases for every year you have worked in the business up to a maximum of ten years.

Any gain up to £50,000 is exempt and you have 50% relief on next £150,000 of gains.

However, Retirement Relief has been phased out by reducing these limits by 20% per annum each year after April 5 1999, with NO RELIEF AFTER APRIL 5 2003 unless gain arises before then.

Capital gains change

EVERY year you can dispose of things you own up to a limit of £9,200 without having to pay any CGT.
Gains above that will be taxed at 10% up to £1m. Gains over £1m will be charged at 18%.

Free leaflets

THE Inland Revenue publishes free explanatory leaflets – the main ones for pensioners cover:
- ★ Income tax and pensioners (IR121)
- ★ Income tax and married couples (IR80)
- ★ A guide for widows and widowers (IR91)
- ★ Tax allowances & reliefs (IR90)
- ★ What happens when someone dies (IR45)
- ★ Capital Gains Tax (CGT14)
- ★ A guide for people with savings (IR110)
- ★ Inheritance Tax an introduction (IHT3)
- ★ The new ISA – a Guide for savers (IR165)
- ★ Self assessment – your guide (SA/BK8)

Chapter eight
YOUR SAVINGS
Defending your family assets

IN THE past people relied on tins – one for the gas bill, another for groceries and the most neglected of all for any savings. These days everything is far more sophisticated. For a start a series of tins like this is a huge temptation to passing burglars and, just as important, the money in them does not earn you any interest. And when inflation goes up, your money decreases in value. Properly invested, it not only keeps pace with inflation but it can earn you a little something on top, too.

But where you should put it can be very confusing. As you hit retirement you will be bombarded with ideas for ways to invest your money, all billed as "foolproof" and often using jargon that most of us without a degree in economics cannot understand at all.

Only you can decide what's best and your decision will obviously have to be based on how much actual cash you have. If you have a fair bit you may decide to go for safety for most of it – and then use a little to do something more adventurous.

Just don't put all your eggs in one basket – spread the risk, and keep a tight control of it.

DEPOSITS AND INVESTMENTS

A DEPOSIT, according to the dictionary, is a sum placed in a bank, usually paying interest and not allowed to be withdrawn without notice. You put your money in and watch it grow...in a building society, bank or National Savings account.

Investments, on the other hand, are money put in stocks which can also be used for growth if you make the right choice. If you don't your money can actually start to diminish, but if you're lucky, it could do very nicely.

So how do you know what's best for you?

What you need is expert independent advice – and this can be one of the hardest things to find. The Citizens Advice Bureau is certainly a starting point – many areas now have money centres where you can get independent help and they will know about this. Alternatively try the Financial Ombudsman Service (see pages 136-137) for the names of independent advisers in your area.

Think about the kind of investments that interest you most and then try and find a specialist in each field.

Safety first

FOR MOST of us safety means building societies and banks (also National Savings schemes – described later). There is a lot of competition for your savings. A growing number of building societies are now offering high interest-paying accounts worth investigating. Your best bet is to work out how big an investment you can afford to make, whether you plan to save a regular sum each month and decide how long you can afford to lock your money away – and then shop around for the best deal.

You will find there's quite a difference in the accounts offered at various societies. Some pay most on large deposits and a minimum balance of, say, £10,000 for their top yielding account, while others will let you benefit like this for an initial stake of £250 and a promise to save a fiver a month. Avoid those which charge you if your balance drops below a certain figure.

The reason for this is pure competition. Nowadays, say some financial advisers, many of the real bargains are to be had with the smaller societies. Their overheads are lower – with only a few offices in the country instead of hundreds.

The banks have not been slow to respond to the competition from building societies. As a result some now offer a no charges deal for customers in credit, even paying interest on current accounts.

Whatever you decide to do, the secret is to make the best use of the services each offers, get them to work for you and keep in control.

With the abolition of composite rate tax in April 1991, savers who are non-taxpayers can now register to get their interest on savings without paying any tax on form IR85 from your building society, or reclaim any that has been deducted.

It is worth moving assets that earn interest to a wife if she has insufficient income to make full use of her tax allowances. If she then registers as a non-taxpayer, she will receive the interest gross.

PEPs, TESSAs AND ISAs

Since April 5 1999 you have no longer been able to invest in PEPs (Personal Equity Plans) and TESSAs (Tax Exempt Special Savings Accounts); they have been replaced by Individual Savings Accounts (ISAs) – see below.

But that does not mean you have lost the tax benefits of PEPs and TESSAs from previous years. If you took out a TESSA before April 5 1999 it will still continue accruing interest tax-free until its five-year term is up, as long as you do not make any withdrawals. Once it has matured, you will be able to re-invest the capital tax-free into the cash element of an ISA, on top of that year's ISA cash allowance. An investment known as a TESSA – only ISA.

The dividends and any capital growth on PEPs you took out before April 5 1999 will also retain their tax-free status until you dispose of them.

Since 6 April 1999 however tax-free dividends have become less attractive for both PEP and ISA investors because from that date the tax credit that fund managers can reclaim on dividends from UK shares was cut from 20% to 10% and in April 2004 it disappeared entirely.

If you are not happy with the way your PEPs are performing or you have a mixed bag of PEPs taken out in different years, you can switch fund managers or consolidate your holding even though PEPs are no longer open for new investments. Take great care that you don't inadvertently sell your PEP rather than transferring to another manager.

If you have been saving regularly into a PEP your fund manager will probably try to make the transfer as smooth as possible.

ISAs

The Individual Savings Account (ISA for short) is the new tax-free savings scheme that took over from the existing PEP and TESSA schemes on 6 April 1999. The Government has said ISAs will be available for at least 10 years.

Returns from ISAs are free of income tax and capital gains tax; you don't have to declare your ISA income or gains on your tax return and you can get your money out at any time without losing tax relief.

You save through an ISA manager, such as a high street bank, insurance company or fund manager. Your money can go into cash, stocks and shares, and some specially-designed life insurance policies.

NEW RULES – From April 2008 you can put into an ISA £7,200 per year including £3,600 cash. You can also move savings held in a cash ISA into Stock and Shares ISAs, but not the other way round. The rules are simpler – anyone over 18 has an annual ISA allowance of £7,200. Up to £3,600 of that may be saved in cash with one provider. If you wish you can put the whole £7,200 into stock and share. 16-18 year olds can save up to £3,600 in cash ISA, but cannot hold stocks and shares. If you feel the stock market is for you, you can now transfers some of your previous cash ISA savings into the stocks and shares ISA, but whatever you do – watch out for exit penalty charges.

The Government has introduced voluntary CAT standards (it stands for fair Charges, easy Access and decent Terms) for ISA managers. It says the standards are intended to help inexperienced investors find straightforward products which offer a reasonable deal. However, a CAT standard ISA does not guarantee a good investment performance, and not having CAT standard terms does not necessarily mean an ISA is a bad deal.

Like PEPs, stocks-and-shares ISAs are likely to be most suitable for higher-rate taxpayers and those who can afford to invest the full allowance each year in successive ISAs.

The less-well-off investor will find the management charges more onerous and is less likely to have any liability to CGT, so gets no benefit at all from that exemption.

If you are attracted to the stockmarket it makes sense to hold your investment within an ISA, but remember that performance is more important than tax perks, and again it is important to take a hard look at the management's investment record before making a choice. Expert help is also advisable in choosing the right ISA, for instance whether you are looking for long-term capital growth, income, or a safer deposit-based account.

NATIONAL SAVINGS

THE days when you used to stick a 6d stamp on a National Savings card are long since gone.

Nowadays there are lots of schemes to choose from, often with the important advantage to many pensioners of paying interest without deduction of tax at source.

The precise conditions of who can hold what and of which account pays which rate vary. But the different National Savings accounts, bonds and certificates tend to rise and fall together.

The big advantage, of course, is that whichever plan you choose, your capital is safe and if you do not pay income tax and are on a low income, then even lower than average interest rates can currently still represent a good deal.

National Savings has a good line-up of products, starting from the

Easy Access Savings Account which has replaced the Ordinary Account. Farther up the scale are the ordinary NS certificates and the index-linked certificates, the latter protecting capital against inflation so that although you don't win apart from an added bonus, you can't lose either, except what you might have gained if your money had been invested elsewhere. They pay a set rate above inflation.

Interest on all issues of National Savings Certificates is completely free of tax. Other National Savings schemes are Premium Bonds, which offer monthly prizes but no interest and Pensions Guaranteed Income Bonds paying interest gross.

Capital Bonds currently offer annual compound interest, guaranteed for five years, paid gross, and so are suitable for non-taxpayers.

Income Bonds, paying gross interest monthly on the 5th of each month, are also suitable for non-taxpayers.

The Investment Account, operated through the Post Office, pays gross interest on amounts from £20 to £100,000.

For anyone whose income is above their personal allowance, and who is therefore a taxpayer, tax will be due on the gross income received from the National Savings Investment Account, Capital Bonds, or Income Bonds. Interest must be declared on your annual Income Tax return.

The First Option Bond gives a fixed rate of interest, set for a year at a time from the date of purchase. Interest is paid net of basic rate tax, which is taken off before you receive it.

The Pensioners' Guaranteed Income Bond is now available to anyone aged 60 or over and offers a monthly income, paid gross on interest rates fixed for a five-year period. It is designed to help overcome some of the difficulties people experience in budgeting for retirement when interest rates on savings are moving up and down. National Savings also offers two and five year Pensioners Bonds, available from post offices. Interest is fixed over the term, and married couples can hold up to a maximum of £1 million.

Main Post Offices have details and booklets about all National Savings accounts.

Moving out of one issue into a more recent one can pay off,

depending on the interest advantage and how long you have held your savings. For information ring 0645 645000.

Unit trusts and investment trusts

IF YOU fancy investing in the Stock Market, many financial experts see Unit Trusts or Investment Trusts as excellent ways for the newcomer to begin.

It is only fair to point out that these were affected in the great Stock Exchange crash when millions of pounds were wiped off the value of Unit Trusts and Investment Trusts, along with everything else. So you would still be taking a risk.

What the building society quotes you will actually get, whereas with a Unit Trust or Investment Trust you could get a lot more. On the other hand you could get a lot less!

Unit Trusts and Investment Trusts are basically baskets of stocks and shares usually held in a particular field of investment or invested in a particular area of the world and managed by a specialist company.

Unit Trusts are set up under trust deeds approved by the Government. As soon as the units are put together, they are offered for sale by the trust managers whose job it is to manage them successfully in order to produce a profit.

They must also promote the fund in order to attract more money to create additional units. In effect this creates a large pool of money to buy shares while allowing the individual investor in the fund to come in and out of it easily.

Investment Trusts operate in a similar way but are themselves companies, governed by company law, which hold and manage the shares of other commercial enterprises.

Of course, the success or failure of a particular fund depends on the investment skill of the managers who actually choose the investments as well as managing the fund. Over the years they build up a considerable degree of knowledge in their specialist area.

There are now a number of different categories containing nearly 1,800 different trusts.

At any one time the monthly league tables published in the

financial pages of the national press will show the best and worst performers in particular sectors, together with the sector average.

Experts say you should not take too much notice of a fund's past performance – when you are buying what matters is the future performance and price. Get expert advice if you are not sure.

Income is paid net of basic rate tax in the form of dividends, but non-taxpayers can reclaim the tax paid. Higher rate taxpayers will have to pay more, of course. The minimum investment varies from trust to trust and it is possible to spread an investment of, say, £1,000 across as many as 400 companies.

Again, experts think it is better when spreading the risk to select from more than one sector of Unit Trust or Investment Trust.

That's because sometimes one sector hits a bad spot and underperforms for a long time. By having your money in different sectors this shouldn't cause you so many problems.

You usually buy direct from the Unit Trust houses or the Investment Trust managers, or you can use the services of a professional adviser – try to find someone who is genuinely independent. If you work for a big company someone there may be able to advise on this, or ask friends and relations.

SHARES

ONE IN four of us now have shares, often in the form of Unit Trusts as already described, or through a PEP, or ISA.

Lots of people start investing in shares at work. Many large companies have schemes whereby employees save regularly in a save-as-you-earn scheme and then after a set period are allowed to use the money to buy shares in the firm.

But the fact is that unless you are very well off, most financial experts do not regard the eve of retirement as the time to start playing the stock market, with the exception perhaps of certain privatisation issues.

GILTS

THEY may sound like something only for the very rich, but anyone with a bit of capital could consider investing in gilts.

They are in fact stocks issued by the Government as a way to fund spending, offering a fixed rate of interest and redeemable after a set time or on a specific date.

There are lots to choose from, each with their own individual characteristics, which makes for a complicated choice for the small investor. However, they are usually issued in blocks of £100 – though just to add to the confusion this is not what you actually pay but what you get back when you redeem them.

The rate of interest varies and the redemption dates do too – some have a date of less than five years away while others can run for 15 years or more.

Some Government stocks are linked to the cost of living. They work in the same way as the normal gilts but the nominal value and interest payments increase in line with inflation.

Which kind is best for you can sometimes depend on your tax situation, as income tax is payable on this interest.

You can buy gilts through the medium of a Unit Trust or alternatively you can use a stockbroker which will involve you in paying commission.

INSURANCE

MANY experts see life assurance as being one of the most effective ways of saving over your working life. Such schemes have been running for many years and can be useful to someone who needs a regular income.

What these schemes do is tie up your money for a number of years and the capital investment is then used to buy you a temporary annuity – that's a special investment which gives you a proper income of a set amount at regular intervals.

Part of what you pay goes to an endowment assurance policy and this combination provides both for a net income and the capital repayment, provided the plan is maintained for the full term.

You could also consider using your retirement tax-free lump sum to buy an annuity, which will give you an income for the rest of your life. This option is less attractive at the moment as annuity rates are at an all-time low. The amount you will get depends obviously on the amount invested, but will be affected by your age and general state of health. Also, whether you want a "guaranteed period" (meaning your annuity will be paid for a minimum length even if you were to die in the meantime), a pension for a surviving spouse, and an element of inflation-proofing.

INVESTMENT 'ADVISERS'

THERE are many different savings and investment schemes on offer nowadays, and an even larger number of 'financial advisers' eager to help you choose the right one, and earn commission from your investment!

It's important, therefore, to choose the right adviser if you're to protect yourself from the rogues and incompetents that, sadly, still exist.

Many so-called advisers are simply salesmen concerned with only one company's products. They are called "tied" agents. That doesn't necessarily have to be a bad thing, but make sure you ask any adviser you consult whether he is "tied", or totally independent, in which case he can offer you products from the whole market place.

The adviser to avoid at all costs is the one who lives only for today and is concerned more with the commission he'll earn on the insurance or investment product he sells you than whether it is, in fact, the best one for your personal circumstances.

To safeguard yourself, make sure that any adviser you contact is a member of the Financial Ombudsman Scheme.

For more details contact the address at the end of this book.

Anyone in the business of giving financial advice or selling investments must be a member of the FOS.

'BEST' ADVICE

TO DO their job properly, good advisers need to ask questions about your financial situation, some of which you may find rather personal.

You don't have to answer all the questions, but it's in your interest to do so as advisers are duty-bound to give you the "best advice" they can.

Once they have all the relevant information, the adviser will put together a suitable investment package for you. If they are "tied" agents they will obviously have to try to do this from that company's products. But if there is nothing suitable for your requirements in that range, they must tell you so and not fob you off with the next best thing.

Once your requirements have been met, the company must send you a customer agreement setting out the services it is providing and the fee it is charging. Don't sign on the dotted line unless you agree with this.

If you are subsequently unhappy with the way you have been treated, then you can complain. Not covered under the complaints procedure, of course, are the usual risks of investment.

But for the unfortunate savers who lose their money in an authorised firm that defaults or goes bust, there is some compensation available from a special fund known as the Investors' Compensation Scheme.

A debt of up to £30,000 can be claimed in full. And if you are owed more than this, you can also claim 90% of the next £20,000. This means that the scheme is normally able to pay out up to £48,000 to each individual.

BUDGETING

EVEN if you've never needed to stick to a budget before, it's vital that in retirement you identify just what your new income and expenses will be, and decide what you will do with any lump sum, matured endowment policy proceeds or inheritance you receive.

Then you can spend, spend, spend – or save, save, save depending on your plans. No matter what age you retire, it's important to recognise that while you won't be as well off as on a salary, your commitments may well be less. But bear in mind that certain options close with your final day at work. While you are still employed, it is easier to increase your working income. Your pension, however, may well fall behind the cost of living.

When you share your life with a family or partner, it is important to be open about the true state of your financial affairs. Then neither of you will be tempted to overspend, trying to keep up with former colleagues still on salaries, or rein in too tightly and skimp unnecessarily. Any budget you devise should include an element of investing for growth so that you can maintain the lifestyle you enjoy for as long as possible.

Remember that as a pensioner some of your savings may involve interest which is paid to you "gross", that is BEFORE tax has been taken off. This particularly applies to some of the National Savings schemes.

In these cases you will have to pay the tax you owe at the end of the tax year, and so it is important to include in your personal budget a reserve for tax not already taken off your savings or investment interest before you receive it (see Budget Planner, right).

On the plus side of your budget, you'll have your occupational pension and a State pension, and you will be relieved of the burden of contributing to your pension fund and National Insurance. If you opt to take a lump sum from your pension fund, you won't pay tax on it – but your pension will be reduced accordingly.

BUDGET PLANNER

ITEM	BEFORE RETIREMENT	AFTER RETIREMENT

INCOME BEFORE TAX:
Employment
Investments
Pensions
Any other source

Total

EXPENDITURE
Taxes – reserve for tax not already taken off
National Insurance
Pension scheme contributions
House insurance, inc contents
Life insurance
Others (not car)

House:
Council Tax
Water rates
Rent or mortgage repayments
Heat and light
Repairs, decoration
Household goods
Furniture and carpets

Transport:
Fares
Car tax
Car insurance
Car maintenance
Petrol and oil
AA/RAC subs

Continued overleaf

ITEM	BEFORE RETIREMENT	AFTER RETIREMENT
Food and drink: At home Away from home Pet food and vet bills		
Entertainment: Papers, periodicals, books Sports and hobbies Theatre, cinema TV rental/licence Club subscriptions Classes & courses Holidays		
Personal spending: Hair and beauty Clothes, cleaning & repair Cigarettes and tobacco Confectionary Beverages Betting Charity Post and telephone **Other**		
Miscellaneous: Cards and presents Chemist Prescriptions Dentist Optician Other Reserve for emergencies and unexpected items		
Other		
Total		

Chapter nine
MOVING ON OR STAYING PUT

Make the right decision on where to live

GIVING up work often goes hand in hand with realising that retirement dream of moving to a little cottage in the country or in the sun of Spain or France.

Of course, this means leaving behind the home you have lived in for most of your working life, no doubt originally chosen for its proximity to the station or motorway rather than the roses growing over the door.

The only trouble is that your retirement choice of area is likely to be the same as that of many other pensioners. And this can produce a massive demand for social services which means a fall in standards...waiting lists for operations like hip replacements are always much longer in these areas, for instance.

Another problem is that the price of homes in these areas is often much higher than you expected, forced up by the competition. You could find that, far from helping you to raise some extra cash, selling up and moving to a popular retirement area actually leaves you out of pocket.

Alternatively, that tiny cottage with roses round the door may be at the top of a hill, in a remote village with few facilities, a very limited social life and no bus service.

The steep staircase which now forms part of its charm may well not seem quite so charming as you grow older.

What suits you now may not seem so attractive when you reach 80 or 85.

Check it all out

TRADING down from a larger to a smaller property can still make good financial sense, choosing whether to move or to stay where you are when you retire is a much more complex question than it appears at first. The type of house, its internal arrangements, the closeness and standard of social and medical services, the proximity of good shopping and what the public transport system is like all play an important part.

Remember, too, that the costs of moving may come to as much as a tenth of what you are paying for your new home and you could end up spending even more of your profit on decorating and furnishing.

Even if you are prepared for these costs you won't be able to keep on moving and facing them again, which is why whatever you decide to do on retirement requires such a lot of thought.

Just as important as the kind of place you decide to live in is how far away the chosen location is from your present address. It's easy to be dismissive about the part family, friends and even neighbours play in your life, but they are important and you will miss them all if you go too far away.

Of course you will make other friends, but if you have lived in one place for very many years it might not be quite as easy as you thought.

You should also make a list of all the other things that are important to you. If you are "townie" for instance, you will not only be used to public transport – even if you have a car now you may not always be able to use it – but also to having shops, libraries and other facilities within walking distance.

There could be a local theatre or cinema, for instance, which once you are retired you could make more use of… such things are less likely to be found in country districts.

You will also be more used to noise and bustle than you realise – the peace of the countryside can sometimes seem almost sinister in contrast. Of course, each case is different, but before you come to any sort of final decision try to put yourself in the position of someone on their own, with no car and restricted mobility for whom outside interests are crucial.

When there's no choice

OF COURSE not everyone is able to consider moving, particularly those in rented accommodation. And even if you own your own home, the prospect of a smaller income may make staying put difficult, if not impossible.

These days lots of us are what the economists call asset-rich, cash-poor. Our basic cash pension will just about cover our everyday needs, while our homes have appreciated to a handsome five-figure sum we can't get our hands on.

But it is possible to realise a large part of the value of your present home and there are some simple ways to use it to raise money.

One of the easiest is to let part of it out. Provided you continue to live there you should not run into any capital gains tax problems. Renting provides a useful source of income and, for those living on their own, some welcome company too.

You would have to declare any rental income for income tax, of course, but you are now allowed to receive up to £4,250 per year from letting rooms, without paying any more tax on it. But do bear in mind that this could affect any Social Security benefits you are claiming.

If you do decide to take this step make sure any lodger you accept has been thoroughly vetted – go by personal recommendation only.

Let for no more than six months to start with, in case you change your mind and, most important, see that you understand all the legal implications and the terminology involved. Your Citizens Advice Bureau should be able to help here.

For a few, one stage up from taking in lodgers is to rent out part of their home as a separate flat, either by converting it or by making use of one which is already there.

You become the "granny" as it were and take over the granny

flat. It does not particularly matter whether the accommodation is furnished or unfurnished since, under the latest Housing Act, you should be able to repossess the property either way – though you must get proper advice on this.

Your lodger becomes a tenant with certain rights whilst you are a landlord with certain responsibilities. You can, for instance, be forced by the local authority to carry out essential but expensive repairs.

UNLOCKING THE CASH

THERE are other ways of raising money on your own home while still living there. Home Income Plans are specifically designed as a way of unlocking useful capital while allowing you to stay put. Of course, there is a price to pay – the two main types of plan on offer will make a big hole in your "estate".

But both are worth investigating as a growing number of retired people living in expensive homes are struggling to make ends meet, and this is one way of making the most of what they own.

However, if you do decide to take things further, make sure you consult your family and a solicitor. If you haven't already got one, ask friends for personal recommendations or contact your Citizens Advice Bureau – the address is in the phone book.

THE HOME INCOME PLAN is currently the most popular scheme and is also sometimes known as a Mortgage Annuity.

Basically this means that a loan (or mortgage) is given to you against your home and the money is used to buy an annuity – a special investment which gives you a yearly income of a set amount, in this instance guaranteed for life.

As well as the money that comes regularly to you, another part of the income from the annuity goes to pay off the interest on the loan.

In other words, this is rather like a second mortgage. Because your home is still yours it is you who benefits from any rise in house prices.

The original loan does not have to be repaid during your lifetime but is repayable on death – or, with a couple, on the death of the survivor. The minimum age to qualify for a plan is 69, but if you are a couple then your combined ages must total 145.

How much money you can raise for the company to buy your annuity is generally limited – somewhere between £15,000 and £30,000.

However, if property prices rise, the scheme offers facilities to increase the income you get.

But you never get a loan invested on your behalf that's worth the full value of your home – it's usually around a maximum of three quarters of what it's worth.

Though most plans refer to houses, you can be eligible if you live in a flat or maisonette, provided you have a long enough lease. It is only if you have tenants or some other outstanding loan that you may be turned down.

As the plans are all about risk, the odds are you will be offered more income the older you are.

Sometimes you may also be able to get an immediate cash sum. This will mean less money every month and most experts recommend caution over this.

And what if a policy holder died early, well before he or she had benefited from the annuity but still with the loan left to repay?

Some plan organisers have thought of this and often offer special capital protection option policies which, while reducing the income a little, do at least ensure that your "estate" needs to repay only a proportion of the sum borrowed in such situations.

Nevertheless, because some part of the loan is repayable on death it means what's available to be passed on to the family is obviously reduced.

As far as tax is concerned, basic rate tax payers will receive the income after tax has been deducted at source.

Such plans will not affect the tax you pay on your present income, so this is good news for those in higher tax bands. If you don't pay any tax at the moment you can often get the income without the tax deduction, which obviously improves the benefit, so check this out carefully. Home Income Plans have been made less attractive since the abolition of MIRAS.

HOME REVERSION SCHEMES are different because you actually sell all or part of your home in return for a cash sum plus the lifetime right to continue living there.

But the valuation of your property on which the cash sum is based will appear to bear little relationship to the current market value.

A £100,000 home, for instance, will only raise about £50,000 as a home reversion. The money you get would depend on your age. For instance, a woman of about 66 would receive around 34% of the value whereas a woman of 85 would get about 60%.

The valuation is based on how long the company calculates you will stay there as a sitting tenant paying them nothing in return.

Some schemes are much better than others and build in safeguards that enable you to benefit from any future increase in the property's value, even if you no longer own it, through some sort of profit-sharing scheme.

It goes without saying that it is more important than ever to get proper legal advice on schemes like this. For example, it is crucial to check the terms of the lease regarding your security of tenure.

While you get a bigger cash sum from these schemes than you do with the home income plans, you are giving away a lot more in return. And the money can be invested to provide you with an annuity income if you prefer. If you take a capital sum your tax position would depend on where you invest the money.

QUESTIONS YOU SHOULD ASK

AS WITH anything involving money and where you live, there are all sorts of hidden dangers with these schemes. There are others not featured here where the loan actually increases as the years go by and the interest rolls up. Instead of giving the home owners cash for the rest of their lives they actually end up owing a lot of money.

Before you consider using your home as a way to raise some income you must get independent financial advice. If you don't know how to find this then go to your Citizens Advice Bureau or Legal Advice Centre – you'll find the address in your phone book or from your local library.

You could also contact Age Concern at 1268 London Road, London SW16 4EJ. Tel: 020 8679 8000. They publish an excellent guide to "Using Your Home as Capital" by Cecil Hinton.

You must also use the solicitor of your choice, not one acting on behalf of the people selling you the plan. And before you do anything check out the following questions:

- What happens if you want to move? This is possible with a Home Income Plan.
- Are you receiving any kind of State Benefits that would be affected by an improvement in your financial situation? If you lose them as a result will the money you get from the plan make up for this?
- Do you know all the costs involved? Administrative fees, legal costs, insurance and, most important of all, who is responsible for them? Are any refundable later?
- Have you sorted out the tax situation? Not all the schemes work to your advantage on this.
- Is the company you are considering a member of Safe Home Income Plans (SHIP) Contact them at PO Box 516, Preston Central, Preston, PR2 2XO, Tel: 0870 341 6060, E-mail: info@ship-ltd.org, Website: www.ship-ltd.org, for members.

PAYING THE BILLS

WHETHER you decide to move or to stay put you will still have to meet the bills for repairs and improvements plus heating out of a reduced income. That's why it can pay to investigate the grants that are available for major structural work, plus insulation, that in turn will reduce your heating costs.

The rules and conditions under which improvement grants are made vary, depending on where you live as much as on the work to be done. Most are given at the discretion of the local authority, but anyone over the age of 60 can apply for a grant towards loft and draught insulation, although this grant is means-tested. Call 0800 181667 or log on to www.eaga.co.uk for more details.

Retirement homes

SPECIAL retirement homes are big business now. In the past sheltered housing, as it was called, was provided by local authorities, charities and housing associations and nearly always involved long waiting lists.

But these days, easy-to-manage, purpose-built and self-contained units are on offer in the private sector for people of an independant nature.

The aim of these places is to give as much independence for as long as possible in a safe, secure environment, avoiding the institutional feel of the traditional old people's home. The help on offer is discreet – someone to turn to in an emergency as well as a good security system.

If you do decide to consider such a place, when you visit look out for the tell-tale signs of a hastily conceived development... the steps where there should be ramps, the lack of hand rails, badly sited lighting or high kerbs.

None of these things may be a problem to you but they say a lot about the amount of thought that has gone into the development.

Retirement homes are certainly not cheap. There is usually a lower age limit of, say, 55 for prospective buyers and any money left over from the sale of your former home may have to be put aside to cover service charges which, not surprisingly, tend to be high. There is often an obligatory fee to be paid, of around 1% of the sale price, when you come to sell.

Retiring abroad

SELLING up and taking the first plane out to settle somewhere exotic is a retirement dream many of us share. It can work... but only if you do your planning carefully.

You need to know not only if you can draw your State Pension in the country of your choice, but also who will look after you as you grow older, what medical facilities are available if you become ill and how you will make yourself understood.

The basic State Pension may not seem much but it is linked to the cost of living and often forms a major part of a pensioner's income.

The fact is there is no difficulty getting it paid anywhere in the world provided you notify the Department of Social Security's special overseas branch in Newcastle in advance of emigrating. They can then arrange for it to be paid to you in the location of your choice in much the same way as through a Giro here.

However, there are problems in some countries – Canada for instance – where your pension is paid but only at the rate applying when you left the UK.

In other words, if you leave this year and are getting the current pension for a couple, that is what you will still be getting in 10 years.

So it is effectively frozen from that time on, with no cost of living or further increases.

The good news is you can get these increases in countries where the UK has a reciprocal agreement – this includes all our European Community partners. The list also includes Bermuda, the Channel Islands, Switzerland and the USA.

Company pensions have no restrictions on where they can be paid either, but should the two when added together put you into a basic tax bracket, there are certain steps you will have to take in order to satisfy the Inland Revenue as to your overseas status.

You will need to get expert advice on this, but a lot depends on whether you plan to return home from time to time – and most important, whether you keep a place in the UK in which to stay.

Once you do this you will be deemed resident here for any year in which you return, however short your stay, and whether or not you own the accommodation. Your best bet once you start thinking about emigrating is to get help...the Citizens Advice Bureau should be able to suggest a suitable expert or you may find your bank helpful here. Both the Inland Revenue and the DWP have leaflets about retiring abroad.

THEM AND US

IF YOU think our tax system is complicated, just wait till you see what faces you in some of the countries where you may be considering retiring! Who would know, for instance, that French death duties vary conversely with the proximity to the family?

The closer the relatives are the less they have to pay, starting with the spouse. Second cousins twice removed are treated very differently from sons and daughters.

Portuguese rates, on the other hand, are two-tiered with one part payable on the land based on a percentage of its value and the other on the rent from or the assessed rentable value of the property at a higher percentage .

All this makes doing your home work about life in the country of your choice so important. Start in the UK with the embassy information service and the commercial attache. It is the latter who will have more day-to-day British contacts, will generally speak better English and will certainly be the best informed about the tax and legal situation in his or her own country.

Chapter ten
SORTING OUT YOUR AFFAIRS

Your inheritance checklist

ONLY one in four of us ever get around to making a will... and one reason is that lots of us genuinely believe we haven't anything to leave.

But the fact is we all have something... anyone who owns a house, for a start, probably has a very considerable amount. But even if you aren't a property owner you might have a gold watch, your own car or even some money in the bank.

Others assume a will isn't necessary because his or her partner will automatically inherit the lot. But this doesn't always happen – sometimes a couple die together, for instance – and in any case it will still involve those who are left in a lot of complicated work during their time of mourning.

What a will does is make it clear exactly what is to happen to your "estate" – the legal term for the value of all your assets once any tax, debts and funeral expenses have been paid.

In addition a will appoints the people you choose to sort everything out for you, called your executors, as well as making any special requests for sums of money to go to, say, a pet cause once all your immediate family has been taken care of.

GETTING ADVICE

MOST stationers and even some post offices have special forms you can fill out at home when you come to make your will, but even so it's still very easy to make mistakes.

For instance, two witnesses are required by law when you actually sign your will and they must be there together – if one went to answer the door then, strictly speaking, the will would no longer be valid.

What's more neither of the witnesses must be beneficiaries in any way or they would not be allowed to receive whatever you had left them. And this also applies to the husband or wife of those witnesses, because he or she benefits indirectly.

There are other potential pitfalls too. Even though the witnesses do not need to know what the will contains, for instance, a blind person is disbarred. And should you have second thoughts and want to amend the will on the spot, all three of you would have to sign the amendments.

Lots of people also go wrong in the way they phrase their bequests – they get the name of the charity slightly wrong or they leave their "favourite" necklace to someone without describing it in more detail and then no-one can remember which one it was.

Pet names for members of the family can also cause problems – one man left everything to "mummy", but he called his wife by this name as well as his mother who was still alive at the time.

Another potential problem is that the law of inheritance and wills is different in Scotland from that in England and Wales. But many of the special will forms designed for English law are sold in Scotland, which can give rise to problems.

The way in which wills need to be signed in Scotland is also different – if the will is in your own handwriting, for example, witnesses may not be necessary.

What to pay

THE simplest way to cut out all this potential hassle is to consult a solicitor. It won't cost you that much and it is a one-off payment. Costs vary depending where you live, and on how complicated your will needs to be.

You may not have to pay anything at all, or certainly only a much reduced fee, to a solicitor who prepares your will if you appoint one of the solicitors at the firm to act as an executor.

A solicitor appointed as an executor will have to be paid for his professional services after your death, though in Scotland it is rare for a solicitor to make any specific charge in relation to his duties as an executor – his charges will relate to the administration connected with the legal work instead.

There are provisions for those on low incomes to be entitled to legal aid and the CAB can explain just who is eligible.

If you are not quite sure about the duties of executors, these are basically the people you appoint to be in charge of your affairs and to see that your wishes are actually carried out.

They start to deal with your affairs from the moment of death. There can be a great deal of work involved, so it is tactful to ask the people you choose, if they're not your solicitor, if they mind before actually naming them in your will.

If you are married and both of you plan to leave virtually everything to each other then you could become each other's sole executor, provided your affairs are straightforward.

The only trouble is that the bereavement itself could make this a particularly upsetting and difficult job.

That's why a better idea can be to also appoint one, competent close friend each to help the survivor sort everything out sympathetically.

Most "estates" are far from complicated but it does help to keep all the relevant papers in one place known to all the family.

PLANNING YOUR WILL

EVEN if you use a solicitor, you still need to work out what you want to happen to your "estate". And there are other things to think about, too.

If you own your home jointly with your spouse or partner under what's legally defined as a "joint tenancy", remember that your co-owner will automatically inherit your share, whatever you say in your will.

If, however, you have a "tenancy in common", then you have the right to leave your share to whoever you want. These terms should have been explained to you by the solicitor when the title deeds were drawn up.

If you have a mortgage, the deeds are held by the building society or bank from where you borrowed the money. You can check the terms there if you aren't sure.

Sole owners of a property can obviously leave it as they choose. Couples in rented accommodation need to check with their landlord or a solicitor what happens if one of them dies.

The surviving partner can almost invariably have the tenancy transferred if they want – but now is the time to make sure.

ALL IN THE FAMILY

YOU also need to think about how you would like your children to benefit. If they are still young they can't actually inherit until the age of 18.

You can specify an even later age if you fear they wouldn't be responsible enough then...lots of people use 21 or even 25 instead.

In Scotland the law on wills is very different, and it should be noted that, even if you leave a will, the law provides that certain relatives may be entitled to claim against your estate contrary to your will. This is not the same as them actually contesting your will.

Accordingly, in Scotland unless your spouse and your children, and the children of any child of yours who has died, is prepared to agree to the provisions in the will relating to them, you are not able to do as you would like.

Nearly all pension plans allow for payments to the surviving widow or widower once the actual recipient dies.

If you aren't married but have a long-term partner you can nominate him or her as a beneficiary. Contact the trustees of the personal pension scheme you belong to – the address should be on the policy document.

You can also leave what's legally known as a "specific bequest" to individual friends or an organisation...for example, a favourite piece of jewellery. If it's a specific sum of money you want to leave then it's known as a "pecuniary bequest".

Both the gift and the chosen recipient should be clearly identified – be sure you have a proper description of the item along with the full address of the person named.

If you have a favourite charity you want to support, it won't just have a name but also a registration number. It pays to use both – your local reference library should have a book containing these or you could contact the charity direct and ask for its details.

THINGS TO THINK ABOUT

IN A will you can say whether you want to be cremated or buried as well as giving details of the way you would like your funeral conducted. You can name a particular church for the service, for example, along with the hymns you would like to have sung or the music you want played.

It's also customary to leave a token bequest to a non-professional executor. If you are worried about the cost of the funeral itself and the worry this might cause your partner, you could consider taking out a funeral payment plan to cover the cost.

But a reminder – if you do take out such a plan, make sure your family know you have done so and with which company.

Once all your wishes have been carried out and all expenses have been deducted what's left is called your residuary estate. The last thing you have to decide is who you want to receive or share in this.

Then once your will has been drawn up for you by a solicitor you must decide where it should be kept.

It's a good idea to keep a copy of it with all your documents, like birth and wedding certificates, for instance. With it there should be a note saying where the top copy is – probably safest with the solicitor who drew up the will for you in the first place, or your bank.

CHANGING YOUR WILL

YOU can change your will as often as you like...the valid one is the last one you ever make.

For single changes like an extra bequest or an update on the money you wish to leave, all that's needed is a "codicil", which is the legal term for an amendment. However, because it is a legal document it must be signed and properly witnessed.

When more substantial changes are involved it's probably easier to draw up a new will altogether, but again it makes sense to seek legal advice.

A will is automatically cancelled – or revoked, to use the correct legal term – on marriage in England and Wales, unless it was drawn up specifically with a marriage in mind.

This does not, however, apply in Scotland.

With a divorce after a will has been made, then legally it will be interpreted as if your ex-spouse had died on the day your marriage was officially ended. Any gift left to him or her will go to the person who gets the residuary estate.

Again, the position is different in Scotland.

What happens when there's no will?

IF SOMEONE dies "intestate" or without making a will then, in England and Wales, where everything he or she owns actually goes depends on personal circumstances. For instance, if the person was married with children, then the surviving spouse gets the "chattels" or belongings, plus a lump sum up to £125,000.

Anything left over would be divided equally in two – one half invested for the surviving spouse, who will get the interest but not the capital which passes to the children, including illegitimate ones, on his or her death. The other part is given to any adult children or invested on their behalf if they are under 18.

If the deceased person wasn't married or had no children there are laws governing exactly where the "estate" should go.

But by not making a will the family left faces a lot of sorting out. There can be other problems, too. For instance, if the couple have a tenancy in common as opposed to a joint tenancy and one of them dies intestate, the surviving spouse could end up losing their home because it becomes part of the estate to be divided automatically between family members.

A challenge

CLOSE members of your family or other dependants – like someone you live with and support – may be able to challenge your will if you have made no specific provision for them. So if you have strong reasons for feeling that a close family member should not be entitled to anything then an explanatory letter to this effect should be placed with the will.

In Scotland, as already explained, close members of the family have specific claims irrespective of whether or not a will has been made. Challenging a will is, accordingly, uncommon in Scotland.

CHECKLIST

IT HELPS to make a list of what you want to happen before you see a solicitor to draw up your will.

Put down as many details as you can – many solicitors base their charges on time and anything that cuts this down should help you. In particular, be sure to include:

★ **Executors' names and addresses**

★ **Assets:**
  Your house and whether it's owned jointly, rented and so on
  Mortgage details
  Investments and insurance details
  Pension
  Other valuables – car, jewellery, antiques and so on
  Bank and building society accounts and their numbers
  Other savings

★ **Any debts**

★ **Beneficiaries (those you want to inherit)**
  Specific bequests
  Any pecuniary bequests
  Charitable gifts – and check the name and registration number of the charity if you can

★ **Special wishes**

★ **Copies of the will – where do you want them to go?**

Death duties

TIME was when death duties were something you read about in the papers. Only the very rich were involved.

Nowadays it's possible that anyone with a house worth more than £300,000 could be affected. This is the point at which Inheritance Tax can bite into your "estate" at a rate of 40%, meaning your savings and your home. That's why it pays to understand how this tax works and what you can do to ease the burden for your family.

Under present legislation no Inheritance Tax has to be paid on gifts between spouses, either during lifetime or on death, even if the total is more than £300,000. Nor does Inheritance Tax have to be paid on gifts, whatever the amount, to UK-registered charities.

Inheritance Tax used to be known as Capital Transfer Tax, though of course most of us still think of it as death duties. But the fact is it isn't just a tax paid on inheritance when someone dies. IHT may also have to be paid on gifts made during your lifetime.

It's a complicated subject. As a rough guide you need to work out how much your "estate" is likely to be – so add up everything you own – property, cash, savings and investments. If the total looks likely to be less than £300,000, IHT will not have to be paid on your death, otherwise you should start taking some action now.

However, under a new ruling, a married couple have a threshold of £600,000. For example Mrs Smith dies with a small saving of £10,000. Mr Smith dies six month later and can set £590,000 of zero rate allowances against his inheritance tax estate of £610,000. This would mean that tax is only paid on £20,000.

TAX-FREE GIFTS

TO TRIM your "estate" there are tax-free gifts you can make as well as allowances you can use each year.
Every year you can give away tax free:

★ Gifts up to £250 each to any number of individuals.

★ To someone else you can give up to £3,000.

★ Money gifts regarded by the taxman as "normal everyday expenditure". Into this category could come pocket money for your grandchildren or cash sums you use as a way to thank someone in the family – for helping out with the garden, for example.

★ Special occasion gifts are also allowed – you can give an extra £5,000 to your children when they marry and £2,500 when it's each of your grandchildren's turn.

★ Anyone else you know who is getting married can have a gift of up to £1,000 tax-free.

If you have lots of money or property to spare over the IHT limit of £300,000 or £600,000 per couple (which is transferable) it could be worth investigating something called Potentially Exempt Transfers, or PETs, as they are called.

What you do here is to make gifts during your lifetime to reduce the amount you owe when you die – but if you live for at least another seven years after making the gift then you won't have to pay any tax at all.

This can be one way of giving your home to your children. But it isn't that straightforward – there are all sorts of conditions which need going through with an expert.

If you don't know where to go then, again, your Citizens Advice Bureau is a good place to start.

Chapter eleven

ALL IN A GOOD CAUSE

Helping others in your spare time

IF THERE'S one good thing about retirement, it's that it brings with it all the extra free time you want to do the things that you never had time for in the past. But you still want to feel involved and needed.

It's a point well illustrated by the huge numbers of people who get involved with charity work once they've finished full-time employment.

Most of us have a pet cause and at last, in retirement, we can actually devote a lot of time to it.

Voluntary work is one of the most popular areas that people in retirement choose to devote their time to. It's a fact that, today, most charities in Britain are staffed by volunteers...in fact, charity is run by charity.

And these days it's not just flag days and sponsored walks that need organising – fund raising is much more sophisticated and varied, requiring skills that many retired people have to offer.

If you were in management, for instance, you will have all kinds of useful executive experience to offer.

People with personnel experience will be able to help in a charity's more public work. Those with secretarial skills will find that there's always a need for 'backroom' help with the mountains of paperwork that a charity both attracts and generates. And manual workers will find there's no shortage of demand for their practical skills.

Whatever job you did during your working life, there will be something you can enjoy doing in retirement – and you'll have the added satisfaction of knowing that you are really helping a cause you care about at the same time.

It may be that the charity you choose to help is one that you've been helped by, or come into contact with, in the past.

Many of the volunteers who work for the hundreds of medical charities, for instance, have first-hand experience of dealing with the consequences of specific illnesses, while widows form the bulk of those who work for bereavement support groups.

It might be a political party you care about, a specific campaign in your area against a new supermarket, perhaps, or a road that will ruin a particular village or treasured view of the countryside.

Whatever your reasons, your help and vast experience of life will be valued. Charity work is, indeed, one of the most obvious examples of an activity where your age could be used to positive advantage.

What's more this sort of work is a great way to make new friends and replace some of those you had at work – an important consideration.

You'll have the opportunity to mix with people from all different age, social and ethnic groups and will, undoubtedly, find the work both absorbing and stimulating. It will probably be a learning experience, as well!

GETTING STARTED

THE first step if you want to get involved in some charity work is to make a list of exactly what you have to offer. Your skills, your experience, even your hobbies and practical things as well – like being able to drive or cook.

Next work out just how much time you can afford to give – days or hours each week or so much time in a month.

Then find a charity or campaign with which to get involved.

You could write to the head office of your particular favourite – if you don't have the address, ask at the library.

In the letter list the kind of skills you have to offer and the time you can spare. It's best to be honest about this from the start, so no-one enters into the arrangement on false pretences.

Or look in the local paper to see if there are details about planned charity activities in your area or appeals for help.

The following organisations would be delighted to hear from volunteers with free time to help them with their activities:

★ Alcohol Concern, *Waterbridge House, 32-36 Loman Street, London SE1 OEE. Tel: 020 7928 7377.*
★ Amnesty International, *Human Rights Centre, 17 NewInn Yard, London EC29 3EA. Tel: 020 7033 1500.*
★ The Stroke Association, 240 City Road, London EC1V 2PR. *Helpline: 0845 3033 100.*
★ Friends of the Earth, *26-28 Underwood Street, London N1 7JQ. Tel: 020 7490 1555.*

★ National Association of Citizens Advice Bureaux,
115-123 Pentonville Road, London N1 9LZ. Tel: 020 7833 2181.

★ National Association of Leagues of Hospital & Community Friends,
11-13 Cavendish Square, London, W1G 0AN. Tel: 0845 450 0285.

★ National Trust, *36 Queen Anne's Gate, London SW1H 9AS. Tel: 020 7222 9251.*

★ PHAB (Physically Handicapped & Able Bodied Association), *Summit House, Wandle Road, Croydon, Surrey CR0 1DF.*

★ RELATE, *Herbert Gray College, Little Church Street, Rugby, Warwickshire CV21 3AP. Tel: 01788 573241.*

★ Victim Support National Office, *Cranmer House, 39 Brixton Road, London SW9 6DZ. Tel: 020 7735 9166.*

★ Voluntary Service Overseas (VSO), *317 Putney Bridge Road, London SW15 2PN. Tel: 020 8780 2266.*

There are more addresses on page 141.

OTHER WAYS TO HELP

IF YOU decide you haven't as much time to help as you thought, you could make a covenant to your favourite charity instead.

A Deed of Covenant is a legal document used for pledging a certain amount of money regularly to a charity of your choice. You have to commit yourself to pay a fixed amount of money every year – or more often, if you prefer – for a period of at least three years.

But some donors miss out on this because the Deed has not been properly drawn up – it has to comply with the requirements of general non-tax law.

All that is necessary is to complete a legally-effective, simple form and get your signature witnessed by one other person.

The Inland Revenue has designed two simple 'model' forms as guidance – one for England and Wales and the other for Scotland. You will find them at the end of the chapter.

If you follow the wording of these forms when drawing up a covenant then you'll know it will be acceptable to the Inland Revenue. The 'model' deeds are drawn up in 'net' form, which means that you enter on the form the amount of money you actually pay, rather than the gross amount.

If the gift you make to the charity comes out of your taxed income – in other words you have already paid tax on it – then the charity can claim back the tax paid from the Inland Revenue.

You are not normally allowed to receive any benefit in return for your covenant, but some charities do give membership benefits in return for covenanted payments. In the case of ordinary small subscriptions, the benefits available to subscribers are, in practice, ignored by the Inland Revenue if they are worth less than 25% of the subscription.

And if the charity's sole or main purpose is to preserve the national heritage or wildlife, the benefit of a member's right of entry to view the charity's property is left out of the account altogether.

An important consequence of the introduction of Separate Taxation in 1990 is that a husband and wife are now treated separately when they covenant.

TAX-FREE

MONEY given to a registered charity in any form during your lifetime or under your will is always tax-free.

Neither is Inheritance Tax due on payments made for what are deemed "national purposes".

This covers gifts to a favourite museum perhaps or even to a political party, as long as it is one of the main parties. To be classed a main party it must have two MPs in the House of Commons – or one MP plus 150,000 votes at the last election.

If you want to leave money to a pet cause or charity in your will then you should contact its headquarters for details of the kind of legacy you can give.

Again the library should have the address – and most important, where charities are concerned, make sure you get the charity's official number to include in your will so there will be no problems in identifying the charity you mean.

Under the Gift Aid scheme which came into effect in October 1990 there is another way to give cash to a favourite charity and, depending how well off you are, escape some tax at the same time.

The scheme allows charities to claim back the basic rate tax – currently 22% – on donations between £250 and £5 million. And donors in the higher tax bracket, paying at 40%, will then be entitled to claim 18% tax relief on the gift.

Most of those who use the Gift Aid scheme will be people who have had a particularly good year financially but are unsure about the future and, therefore, their ability to continue to make charity contributions in later years.

That's why they would prefer to make a large one-off donation rather than commit themselves to regular giving through, say, a covenant.

We illustrate two versions of a typical Covenant Form, one for use in England and Wales and one for Scotland.

If you want, you can say instead: "for a minimum of four years and thereafter until I terminate this deed."

VERSION A

Form of covenant by an *indivdual to* a *charity* for use *in England and Wales* from 31 July 1990

DEED OF COVENANT

	NOTES
To_____	(Name of Charity)

I promise to pay you for _____ years, or until I die if   **1**

earlier, such a sum as after deduction of income tax at the

basic rate amounts to £ _____   **2**

each [week] [month] [quarter] [year]   **3**

from [the date shown below] [_____]   **4**

Signed and delivered_____   **5**

Date_____

Full Name_____

Address _____

_____

Witnessed by:

Signed_____

Full Name_____

Address _____

_____

NOTES **1.** Enter the period of the covenant, which must be longer than *three* years. **2.** Enter the amount you will be paying to the charity. **3.** Delete as appropriate to show how often you will make the payment. **4.** Delete as appropriate. If you choose to enter an actual date *it must not be earlier than the date you sign the deed.* **5.** You must sign the form and enter the date you actually sign it in the presence of the witness who should also sign where shown.

VERSION B

Form of covenant by an *indivdual to* a *charity* for use *in Scotland.*

DEED OF COVENANT

To_____

NOTES
(Name of Charity)

I promise to pay you for _____ years, or until I die if   **1**

earlier, such a sum as after deduction of income tax

at the basic rate amounts to £ _____   **2**

each [week] [month] [quarter] [year]   **3**

from [the date shown below] [_____]   **4**

Signed_____ Date_____   **5/6**

Full Name_____

Address _____

_____

Witnessed by: **6**

Signed_____ Full Name_____

Address _____

and:

Signed_____ Full Name_____

Address _____

NOTES: **1.** Enter the period of the covenant, which must be longer than *three* years. **2.** Enter the amount you will be paying to the charity. **3.** Delete as appropriate to show how often you will make the payment. **4.** Delete as appropriate. If you choose to enter an actual date *it must not be earlier than the date you sign the deed.* **5.** You must sign the form and enter the date you actually sign it in the presence of the witnesses, who should also sign where shown. **6.** In Scotland *two* witnesses are needed but, if you write the words 'adopted as holograph' above your signature, no witness is needed.

Chapter twelve
STAYING FIT AND FEELING GOOD

It's never too late to feel good

THERE is nothing any of us can do about growing older. But how and when it starts to notice is highly individual. Much depends on genetic inheritance, but even more on general fitness, too. Coupled with this come lifestyle and attitude.

Until recently it was assumed that as people got older they also became mentally less acute, physically weaker and emotionally depressed.

However, this has been shown to be very far from the case. The fact is the more you do, the more you can carry on doing! At the end of the day what matters is your attitude.

When you are at work you have a set routine and a network of friends and acquaintances in which you move. Status and position provide a valuable sense of identity and even if you aren't always in tip-top health, you simply haven't the time to dwell on any problems. The stimulation of work keeps you going.

The trouble is you lose all this the moment you retire, unless you replace the work routine with a whole new range of activities to compensate.

That's why it's important not to underestimate the impact of retirement and to make sure that you are organised in advance with lots of new things to do.

Otherwise, before you know it, you can slip into the "happy doing nothing" lifestyle. The trouble is you probably won't be that happy and the less you do, the less you will want to do.

The secret is not to let this happen in the first place... if you plan well enough ahead you will go straight from one busy life into another potentially equally rewarding one.

Getting used to each other

YOU may have been married for years but the chances are you haven't spent all day and every day together for a very long time! So when you start looking at the future you need to work out a new lifestyle that will suit you both.

Think about retirement as a way of increasing your freedom of choice, giving you both the chance to make new friends, develop new interests and have a great time.

The chances are there are lots of things you talked about doing over the years but never had time for... and this could be the moment.

But it is important to give each other space. If yours is a "traditional" marriage where the husband has gone out to work while the wife stayed at home, a lot of adjustment could be necessary.

The husband who suddenly wants to take over the cooking, for instance, or who starts to question day-to-day household decisions after years of never being involved, could well upset a wife who has always been in charge on the domestic front.

The trouble is she will still have the same routine as she has always had -there will be the shopping to do, the cleaning and the washing. In other words, a wife in this situation may well not see herself as "retired" at all as her life will be just the same as before. And the danger is that real irritation can set in if this fact isn't appreciated.

So what's the solution? To plan for retirement together.

A husband who offers to help with the house as opposed to trying to take over running it, and a wife who becomes less rigid about just what has or hasn't to be done every day, are much more likely to have a happy retirement together.

That's why it pays to make time now to talk through how you see your retirement ... then any problems can be ironed out before they actually happen.

KEEPING BUSY

IT'S A fact that the longer you carry on making maximum use of all your capabilities, from the muscles in your limbs to the memory-storing functions of your brain, then the more slowly you will age.

And this goes for both of you of course – so get out and find something to take up that you will both enjoy.

The trouble is there are lots of myths about retirement and if you don't find something to keep you fully occupied you can end up believing them.

There's the idea that you will need less sleep, for instance, as well the old wives' tale that growing older brings a lot more worry.

In fact, the amount of sleep you need is something that's particular to your own metabolism – if you can't sleep it could possibly be because your bedroom isn't airy enough! Or it could be that boredom has set in and you spend a lot of time nodding off in front of the TV during the evening. By the time you do finally go up to bed you have already had quite a lot of sleep and you are wide awake.

That certainly doesn't have anything to do with age – there are plenty of young executives who do exactly the same every night!

Worry has nothing to do with age either. Retirement itself can bring its own worries – most of which you can do something about. And it's certainly not worth worrying about those things you can't control.

Keep busy, keep interested and you will feel better for it. Set yourself a few challenges . . . vow to learn something new every day and you'll soon feel the benefit.

MAKING NEW FRIENDS

LIKE lots of people, if you rely on work for your social life you need to find other places where you can meet new friends in retirement. The best way is through an interest you already have – whether it's cooking, collecting stamps, playing bridge or joining an amateur dramatic society.

It's best, if you can, to go to places where there's a mixed age group – you don't just want to meet retired people. It's much more stimulating to meet a variety – if you are all the same age the danger is you end up wallowing in nostalgia as well as seeing everything from just one angle.

Don't rely too much on your own children to fill any gaps left by retirement. It may be great to see more of them now you are home all day, but don't spoil a good relationship with them and your grandchildren by relying on them too much.

The fact is your children have made their own lives, in which you obviously feature but can't expect to dominate.

Offers of extra babysitting, if you live close enough, may well be appreciated, but trying to make this your life's work would not be a good idea. For a start, babies have a habit of growing up fast and you could find yourself redundant before you know it.

WATCH WHAT YOU EAT

IT'S A fact that thin people live longer than fat ones – basically because there is less strain on their hearts. So if you are a little overweight, now is the time to lose a few pounds before it becomes a real problem.

Women in particular tend to put weight on as they grow older – their metabolic rate slows so they actually need fewer calories. But as we all know, it's all too easy to carry on eating as before.

There is no need to go on a starvation diet – a sensible eating plan should do the trick. But before you do anything have a word with your doctor first.

It may take a while to lose weight but if you eat sensibly then it should be a permanent loss. Cut out junk food and the empty calories like chocolate, cakes and biscuits and check you are getting enough fibre.

A sensible diet should contain the most important sources of each nutrient.

Every day see you have a serving of at least one of the following – lean meat, poultry, fish or eggs with green vegetables – cooked or in a salad – plus at least one root vegetable such as carrot.

Check your calcium levels – semi-skimmed milk has as much as full cream milk but is lower in fat if you are watching your weight.

Yoghurt is also good.

Try pulses – kidney beans, lentils and so on – as an alternative to meat. Intake of red meat in particular should be watched – choose fish or chicken instead.

Don't be tempted, however, to cut down on the amount you drink – ageing kidneys cannot concentrate urine so well, so it is important to keep up your fluid intake, drinking at least three pints a day.

Alcohol, of course, should be taken in moderation.

And remember that many soft and canned drinks contain a lot of calories – try the low calorie versions of the most common ones for a change.

GETTING INTO SHAPE

OF COURSE, being slimmer doesn't equal being fit. Taking up some exercise is the next step – but it is vital to have a check-up first. It's just possible you could have a hidden medical condition and that embarking on an exercise programme could put you seriously at risk.

There are lots of simple things you can do around the house and garden that can help you get into shape. Experts rate digging the flower beds and mowing the lawn particularly highly in improving the three most important aspects of fitness – stamina, suppleness and strength.

Ordinary walking is great, too – leave the car whenever you can. A brisk walk with the dog is excellent exercise.

Check with your local authority about keep fit classes for your age group. Sports like swimming and golf are excellent – it's things like squash you should give a miss unless you have been playing for years and are confident you are fit enough.

CUT DOWN ON CHOLESTEROL

MUCH is said nowadays about cholesterol, a form of fat found in the blood and certain foods, notably eggs. It can clog the blood vessels, leading to heart and circulatory disease, like angina and coronary thrombosis.

Cholesterol levels can be tested with a free blood test at your GP's surgery. If the test shows that you have a high cholesterol level, a diet avoiding dairy and animal fats is likely to be recommended.

PRIVATE MEDICAL INSURANCE

IF YOU'RE lucky enough to be covered by an employer's private medical insurance scheme while you're working, you'll have to consider whether you can afford to keep up the premiums yourself once you've retired.

As a rule premiums on private medical insurance increase as you grow older, even if you've been in the scheme for some time- it's a sore point that has been the subject of much controversy – and you may find the cost is too much to bear on a restricted retirement income.

It's worth shoppping around, as there are now some special budget schemes designed especially for the over-60s. But make sure any existing condition will be covered if you transfer policies.

No smoking

IF YOU smoke then the chances are that taking up exercise will leave you breathless and puffed out. It's been estimated that you shorten your life by five and a half minutes for every cigarette you smoke.

Yet despite all the overwhelming evidence that smoking is bad for you, more than 50,000 people still die each year from diseases related to cigarettes in Britain alone – the three main diseases relating to smoking are coronary heart disease, lung cancer and chronic bronchitis and emphysema.

Giving it up is a very positive step towards staying fit. For many people cigarettes are part of their routine. They light up at specific times of the day . . . at the morning coffee break, in the pub at lunchtime, for instance.

Retirement can give smokers the chance to break the habit because their routine changes.

When creating a new retirement lifestyle it's possible to design one that doesn't allow for cigarettes at all.

No-one is saying it's easy, but more than eight million people in Britain have managed it!

Most ex-smokers say the only way is to decide on a day on which you will definitely stop smoking, then throw away any cigarettes, lighters, ashtrays and so on. Try and identify the times when you are likely to miss a cigarette most of all – for lots of people it's after a meal or when they pick up the phone. Then you can try to re-organise your life to avoid these situations making you weak-willed.

You may find it helpful to give up with others – there are special groups all over the country you can join for support. Look out for ads in the local paper or ask your GP.

The stress factor

LOTS of people smoke because they feel under stress. It's an increasingly common problem today and it doesn't just occur when people are working too hard.

It's quite possible to feel stressed even if you have very little to do and the best way to relieve stress is to deal with the problems and worries by facing up to them. Talking them through with a neighbour or close friend can help, but do get expert help if things are really getting on top of you. Your doctor should be able to help here. Stress can also be reduced by getting involved in sport, a hobby or some other pastime. The enjoyment factor can help reduce the problem.

Lots of people don't believe it's possible to be stressed and retired at the same time but it most certainly is, especially for those who have given little or no thought to what to do now that work is finished. That's when it becomes vital to find something else to fill the gap.

Check out your health

ROUTINE health checks for men and women are now available every three years, under the new NHS regulations. These checks involve measuring height, weight and blood pressure, together with an analysis of the urine and enquiries about smoking and drinking habits.

Similar checks are likely to be made if you register with a new doctor, and the over 75s should be offered more extensive annual checks, which can take place in their own homes.

In addition, a number of health centres now run "well woman" and "well man" clinics, as well as sessions to help those who want to stop smoking, take up exercise, etc.

Although no-one really enjoys a visit to the doctor, it's important that you take up the offer of these routine checks and attend any special clinics of relevance or interest to you – prevention is better than cure, after all.

The patient and doctor relationship is a partnership that deserves the input of both parties. By showing that you take an active interest in your health, you will, hopefully, get the best out of the partnership.

Checklist

★ One person's 60 is another person's 40. It's not your actual age that matters, but your attitude. Keep your mind alert by learning new things.

★ Don't look ahead to retirement as an end. Instead plan for it by developing a second career or skill. Or try more education – the Open University can be the perfect starting point to learn all the things you have never had time to tackle in the past. And this will all help keep your brain ticking over nicely!

★ Try something new . . . Glasgow, for instance, boasts a highly popular orchestra made up entirely of "retired" people.

★ Make a list before you retire of what you want to do. Include some exercise every day if you can and plan out a proper diet to follow. If you are home more, you might decide to have lunch as your main meal, for instance, and something lighter in the evening. Take a look in the library for healthy eating plans you can follow and devise a few of your own.

Dealing with disability

THE encouraging aspect of dealing with disability – in yourself or in someone you are caring for – is that help is at hand, once you know where to find it.

Not only is free help available through the Health Service and local Social Services, but charities and medical foundations also dedicate themselves to finding cures and helping patients afflicted with ailments, from Alzheimer's Disease to rheumatoid arthritis.

Often, simple adjustments or inexpensive gadgets can make all the difference to coping with the practicalities of life for disabled people. The Disabled Living Centres Council runs over 30 centres from Aberdeen to Exeter where you can try out the latest equipment, helped by experienced staff. Ring 0870 770 5813 for the address of your nearest centre.

If in doubt, ask, demand, bully people into helping you. Make sure you are getting all the aid and State benefits you are allowed, and if you need "Attendance", (ie someone to look after you), or you "attend" someone who needs care, make sure you receive the State support to which you are entitled.

Your starting point is either of the free DWP leaflets: SD1 Sick or Disabled, or SD4 Caring for Someone.

Your own doctor is your first point of contact – his signature will be necessary if you need to apply for a Disabled Person's badge, for example. Even non-drivers who are disabled are entitled to use a Disabled Person's badge in the car of someone able to take them to the shops, Post Office and social events.

Doctors can also recommend treatment, support from Social Services, and the provision of equipment or aids.

Alternatively, ask your local Social Services department to send an occupational therapist to your home to assess the need for home adaptations or mobility gadgets which are available on permanent free loan.

Caring for an old or disabled parent can be more demanding than looking after a sick child.

If you find yourself in this position, take time to assess what their needs are, work out your resources, in terms of accommodation, finances and equipment, and look at what help you can count on from relatives, friends, Social Services and local charities.

Chapter thirteen
GOOD SERVICE

Your rights as a consumer

SHOPPING is something we all do, usually without a second thought – until, that is, something goes wrong. It's important to know your rights as a consumer.

Then if something goes wrong, you'll know what to do about it. Consumer rights are a subject of interest and relevance to all ages. But in retirement they are, perhaps, even more important than ever before – after all, you don't want to waste precious money on and be disappointed by purchases that don't work, break as soon as you've got them home or which are not what you expected.

Your protection as a buyer lies in the Sale of and supply of Goods Act 1994 which covers all goods bought from a trader, whether from shops, street markets, doorstep salesmen, in sales, at parties in private homes, or by mail order.

It doesn't matter whether you pay for goods in cash or by credit – once the seller has accepted your offer to buy, a legally enforceable contract has been made which gives both of you rights and obligations.

Under the Sale and Supply of Goods Act 1994, goods have to be of a "satisfactory quality". This means they have to be durable, safe and free from minor defects.

Also under the Act, you must be able to examine what you buy properly before you lose the right to reject it and claim a refund. So if you buy a lawnmower in the January sales but only discover a fault when you come to use it in the Spring, you will still be able to ask for your money back under the Sale and Supply of Goods Act.

The supply of Goods and Services Act 1982 protects customers who buy a service allied to goods supplied, such as a tiled bathroom or having a house painted.

★ The service must be carried out with reasonable care and skill within a reasonable time and for a reasonable charge.

★ Any materials must be as described and of a satisfactory quality.

You are not entitled to anything if:

★ You examined the item when you bought it, and should have seen the faults then.

★ You were told about any fault – for instance, if the goods were described as "fire damaged".

★ You ignored the seller's skill or judgement as to the suitability of goods for any particular purpose you described to him.

★ You ignored the seller's claim that he wasn't expert enough to advise you correctly about your purchase.

★ You simply changed your mind about wanting the article.

★ You received the goods as a present – the buyer must make any claim.

What to do

IF THERE is a problem with goods you have bought, you should always complain to the seller, not to the manufacturer.

It is a good idea to examine and try out anything you buy as soon as you can. Once you have legally accepted goods which are faulty you lose your right to reject them and are no longer entitled to a full refund.

Acceptance normally means you have kept the goods beyond a reasonable time – you are expected to make it clear to a seller that you are rejecting goods as soon as possible after purchase.

What you are entitled to

PROVIDED you have not accepted faulty goods you do not have to accept a repair or replacement instead of cash compensation.

If you do accept a replacement or repair, write to the shop saying that you reserve your rights under the Sale and Supply of Goods Act to reject the goods – then you can ask for a refund if you are not happy with the repair or if further faults occur.

The shop may offer a credit note instead of a refund in exchange for faulty goods, but you do not have to accept one. Credit notes are sometimes valid for a limited period only, and you may find nothing else you want in that store during that period.

Don't be put off by signs that say "no refunds without receipts" – they do not affect your legal rights and are, in fact, prohibited, so if you see one, tell your local Trading Standards Officer.

Don't be put off either by notices saying "no money refunded", even for sale goods – they are illegal and should also be reported.

Guarantees

A GUARANTEE is always an addition to your legal rights under the Sale and Supply of Goods Act, so your rights are not affected when it runs out. If you're asked to complete and return a guarantee registration card, it's a good idea to do so.

In theory a manufacturer could refuse to honour a guarantee if you did not return the card, though he is unlikely to do so if you have some proof of purchase, such as a receipt.

If a guarantee, or extended warranty, is being sold with the product, make sure you understand what is covered and what is not. Does the price justify the benefits provided?

Secondhand goods

GOODS sold secondhand will probably not be in perfect condition, but they are still covered by the Sale and Supply of Goods Act.

Secondhand goods should still be of satisfactory quality and fit for their purpose, but as with new goods, you can't complain about defects that were pointed out to you or which you should have seen.

If you're buying an expensive secondhand item, take someone with you to note what is said about it by the seller – in the case of cars, it's best to arrange an independent technical inspection before you agree to buy. At the very least, take someone knowledgeable with you if you don't know a great deal about cars yourself.

Sales

SALE items are covered by all the rules in the Sale and Supply of Goods Act – they must be of satisfactory quality and perform the tasks for which they were made.

Buying privately

YOU have fewer rights when you buy something privately, whether it be from a friend, neighbour, or through a newspaper classified advertisement.

The Sale and Supply of Goods Act says that goods bought privately merely have to match their descriptions.

Your other rights will depend on what is said between you and the seller – what you were told about the value of the goods and their condition – so it is a good idea to take along someone who is knowledgeable about the item, or who could act as a witness.

Buying at home

MORE and more people now choose to avoid the hustle and bustle of the big shopping centres and shop instead in the comfort of their own homes. These days you can buy almost anything you want from catalogues, magazines, ordering by phone, or on the internet.

The Sale and Supply of Goods Act covers doorstep salesmen, "party" sales and other traders, and many firms who sell goods in your own home are members of the Direct Selling Association, which has its own code of practice.

Under the DSA code, "party" sales customers have 14 days in which to change their minds about goods ordered and get their deposits back. All sales leaflets must show the company's name and address. Doorstep salesmen covered by the code must carry identification cards and company literature on the products or services offered. Customers also have 14 days to cancel agreements and claim full refunds on deposits.

Buying from a doorstep salesman

REPUTABLE companies, and those which are members of the Direct Selling Association, give their salesmen identity cards, so check he is who he says he is. If you're not interested in what he's offering, say "no thank you" and close the door.

★   Beware of attempts to encourage you to buy in haste, such as one-off discounts or warnings that prices are about to rise. Ask for time to think things over.

★   Find out what similar goods cost in the shops.

★   If a doorstep salesman is trying to interest you in house repairs or improvements, get estimates of the cost from other firms.

★   Never pay in full before receiving the goods or service. If you pay a deposit, insist on a receipt with the firm's name and address on it – and check they are who they say they are.

★   Salesmen may make rash promises to get you to sign a contract, so if you want to order goods only on the condition that they are delivered by a certain time, make sure this is in writing.

★   If you buy something from a doorstep salesman, keep the firm's name and adress in case of problems later.

★ If you're buying on credit, make sure you know the full cost and compare it with other types of credit.

★ If you sign a credit agreement in your own home, you have five days in which you can change your mind and cancel.

★ You have the right to cancel contracts made during a doorstep visit even when no credit is involved, if a trader visits you without invitation or after making a phone call. There is a seven-day "cooling off" period for cash contracts of over £35.

BUYING BY PHONE

PHONE sales are increasingly common – the caller will probably have got your name from the phone book or from one of several lists available to sales organisations.

Reputable companies should:
★ Say who they are, and why they are calling.
★ Phone you before 9pm.
★ Ask if it is a convenient time.
★ Not phone you at work.

If you are not interested, just say so and put down the phone. If you are interested, give yourself time to think the matter over and compare prices.

Never give out your credit or charge card number over the phone to a cold caller or if you have doubts about the firm he claims to be phoning on behalf of.

BUYING BY POST

YOU have the same rights in law when you buy through mail order as when you buy from a shop.

If you buy from one of the large mail order companies which

belongs to the Mail Order Traders' Association you are protected by a code of practice. The MOTA code provides for prompt delivery dates, the return of unwanted or faulty goods, servicing arrangements and a complaints procedure.

Check that delivery costs are included in the overall price when buying from a catalogue.

If you buy something from an advertisement, keep a copy of the advert plus details of your order, how you paid and the date on which you sent it.

Never send cash through the post.

The Safe Home Ordering Protection Scheme and the British Code of Advertising Practice operated by the Advertising Standards Authority cover goods advertised from an advertisement, say in a magazine or newspaper.

The **SHOPS** protects you if you send money for goods to an advertiser who goes into liquidation or bankruptcy before he sends the goods to you.

You have to apply to the Advertisement Manager of the publication which carried the advert within a specified time and you should then get your money back – publications which support a SHOPS carry details about how to claim.

SHOPS do not, however, cover classified advertisements or traders who advertise catalogues from which you have to order goods.

The BCAP requires mail order traders to deliver goods – except plants and made-to-measure items – within 28 days, or tell you if they cannot do so. They must promptly refund your money if you return unwanted goods undamaged within seven days, or if your goods are not delivered within 28 days and you decide you no longer want them.

Who can help?

IF YOU have a shopping problem and can't sort it out yourself, there are several agencies which may be able to help.

Trading Standards Officers investigate complaints and enforce laws relating to false or misleading descriptions of prices, inaccurate weights and measures and some aspects of the safety of goods.

Your local Trading Standards Department is listed in the phone book in the section for your local council, in Northern Ireland under the Department of Economic Development and in Scotland see the entry for your Regional or Island Council.

Often there will also be a consumer credit specialist at the Trading Standards Department, and Trading Standards officers have some responsibility for enforcing the law on some food matters, such as composition and labelling.

Consumer Advice Centres give a wide range of information and advice to shoppers and traders and their staff usually come under the wings of the Trading Standards Department too.

Environmental Health Departments enforce laws covering public health matters, like contaminated food and drink and dirty places where food is stored, prepared and sold.

Their work also covers cleanliness in places used by consumers, such as hair salons.

Environmental Health Departments are listed in the phone book in the section for your local council.

There are around 1,000 Citizens Advice Bureaux which provide independent, free, confidential help and advice on a range of problems.

Some bureaux offer free legal advice and many will agree to act as "go between" in disputes between traders and consumers. They are listed in the phone book under Citizens Advice Bureau.

The Office of Fair Trading publishes a very useful set of leaflets, and the book A Buyer's Guide, which explain consumer rights in more detail.

BUYING ON CREDIT

BUY now, pay later…it seems an attractive offer, and it's one made by all sorts of traders and companies nowadays.

But don't let offers of credit tempt you to buy something you can't afford. You can end up paying up to a third more than if you paid with cash, you'll be committing a chunk of your income for months or even years and, if you can't keep up the payments, you could find yourself in real trouble. It's important, when buying anything on credit, to shop around for the best deal.

If you're being offered interest-free credit, remember to check the obvious – make sure the repayments don't add up to more than the cash price.

And look out for the APR, or Annual Percentage Rate, figures. If the APR is variable the interest rate and your payments can go up or down.

With that in mind, and if your retirement budget is tight, you may feel you'll be better off with a fixed interest loan where you pay the same amount each month.

When you ask for credit, you'll be asked to fill in a form about yourself, your income and outgoings – answer these questions honestly. You'll be doing yourself no favours, but will be breaking the law, if you make out that you're better off than you really are.

Once you've signed, you should get a copy of the agreement, and may receive another in the post. Keep it safely, together with a record of all the payments you make and copies of the statements you receive.

Credit offers often seem more attractive when you're in a shop surrounded by goods than when you're at home and able to take a realistic look at your financial situation. It may be that at a later date you wonder what you've let yourself in for and want to rid yourself of this sort of financial commitment. But not all credit agreements can be cancelled – if you can cancel, there should be a box on the credit form which tells you about this option.

In the main, credit agreements can be cancelled if you met the trader to discuss the deal and signed the form at home.

If you signed in the trader's shop, office or other premises – like on an exhibition stand – you can't usually cancel.

Often people who have bought on credit get tired of being committed to monthly payments and make an effort to pay the balance before the agreement is officially due to end.

If you buy something on Hire Purchase, you can't usually end the agreement unless you're up to date with your payments, and you can't sell HP goods until the agreement has been paid off.

If you want to settle up an unsecured loan early, ask the company how much it will cost in penalty charges – you'll have to pay much of the interest you'd have paid if the agreement ran its full length!

In summary, buying on credit is a good idea only if you fully understand the agreement you are entering into and are sure that you'll be able to keep up with the repayments. In retirement, it may be a good way to spread the cost of an expensive item, but don't overcommit yourself so there's no money left for the little luxuries you've been looking forward to all your working life.

And a final word of warning – if you act as a guarantor for somebody else's loan, you will have to pay all they owe if they stop paying. So don't be a guarantor unless you can afford to take that risk!

Extra protection

IF YOU use your credit card to buy something costing more than £100, you usually have extra protection if something goes wrong.

If, for example, the laptop you bought won't work, you may be able to claim from the credit card company, which is jointly liable with the retailer. Another safeguard is that most items worth more than £50 bought with a card are insured for 100 days, (usually there is a proviso that they are not covered by any other policy). You'll need to supply proof of purchase, though, so make sure you keep copies of all the credit card transactions you make.

For more details, contact your credit card company direct.

Lost cards

AS SOON as you realise that your credit card is lost or stolen, tell the company at once by telephone, then confirm it in writing.

It's vital that you act quickly in these circumstances. You won't be liable for the money spent if someone else uses your card after you've informed the company – but if it's used before then, you may have to pay up to £50.

Keep a note of your credit card numbers in a safe place, in case you ever need to report that they're missing.

Credit card & No:	Contact Telephone No:

Chapter fourteen

USEFUL INFORMATION

Up to date tax tables

State benefit allowances

Organisations and helplines

USE OUR tables to check that you are getting your full tax allowances, including the "Age Allowances" for people over 65, and that you are claiming all the State benefits from Social Security that you are entitled to.

Our address list, starting on page 136, will help you if you need more detailed information.

Personal Income Tax 2008/2009 Rates

£

20% on remaining taxable income per person up to	39,825
40% on taxable income per person over	39,825

Personal Tax Allowances 2008/2009

£

Minimum personal allowance	5,435
Married couple's, allowance (if aged 65 before 5 April 2000)	† 2,540
Blind person, allowance	1,800
Age allowance 65-74:	
Individuals	9,030
Married couple's,*	† 6,535
Age Allowance 75 and over:	
Individuals	9,180
Married couples,*	† 6,625

† *Relief from tax on these allowances is restricted to 10%. The amounts for age-related MCAs were increased in 2003/2004 so that the value of this allowance for people aged 65 or over would be protected.*
* *Husband OR wife over the age limit qualifies for the extra relief.*

Once you are 65, there is an income limit of £21,800 for full relief on your extra Age Allowances. They are reduced by £1 for every £2 your income is over the limit, until you drop to the minimum personal allowance of £5,435 and £2,540 Married Couples Allowance.

Capital Gains Tax

Rates are 10% up to £1m and 18% over £1m in your lifetime.

INHERITANCE TAX

Estate valued up to £300,000 or £600,000 per couple – no tax
Over £300,000 or £600,000 per couple – 40%
100% relief on some business assets and farmland
If you die within seven years of making a gift, its value is added to the value of your estate. Tax is then calculated on a sliding scale:

Up to 3 years	100% of the tax
3 to 4 years	80%
4 to 5 years	60%
5 to 6 years	40%
6 to 7 years	20%

Exemptions and reliefs:	£
Maximum annual gifts per donor	3,000
(previous year's may be used if still available)	
Small gifts per recipient	250
Gifts on marriage:	£
– parent of recipient	5,000
– grandparent of recipient	2,500
– Other	1,000

"HOME INCOME PLAN" RELIEF

From age 65, relief at 23% on £30,000 per person or married couple, if 9/10ths of loan secured on your home is used to buy life annuity, (abolished from 6 April 2000 for all new HIPs).

STAMP DUTY

Buildings and land with sale value between £125,000 and £250,000 = 1%. Buildings and land with sale value between £250,000 and £500,000 = 3% where price is over £500,000 = 4%
On zero carbon emission homes under £500,000 stamp duty is exempt, over £500,000 there is a £15,000 reduction.
Stocks and shares = 0.5%.

Helplines

	TELEPHONE
HELPLINES – UPDATE	
STATE PENSION GUIDE BOOK pensions and widows benefit advice	0845 731 3233
PENSIONERS GUIDE (BROCHURE)	0845 606 5065
ATTENDANCE ALLOWANCE DISABILTY LIVING ALLOWANCE existing claims advice	0800 882200
BENEFITS ENQUIRY LINE benefit advice – disabled and carers	0800 882 200
INVALID CARE ALLOWANCE existing claims advice	0800 882 200
PENSIONS OVERSEAS	0191 218 7777
PENSION CREDITS GUIDE	0845 6065065
WINTER FUEL HELPLINE	08459 151 515
WINTER WARMTH	0800 085 7000
AGE CONCERN	0800 009966
SENIOR LINE benefits advice – Help the Aged	0808 800 6565
NHS DIRECT	0845 4647

CHECK YOUR PAYE CODE

Allowances	PAYE Code ends with letter
Personal Allowance (under 65)	L
Personal Allowance plus Additional Personal Allowance (under 65)	H
Personal Allowance (age 65-74)	P
Personal Allowance (age 75+)	T
Personal Allowance (65-74) plus Married Couple's Allowance (65-74)	V
Personal Allowance (age 75+) plus Married Couple's Allowance (age 75+)	T
If your total income is more than £18,300 per person and you are over 65	T
Over 65 with occupational pension. Where State pension exceeds personal allowances	Starts with K

Main Social Security benefits (per week)

From APRIL 2008

RETIREMENT PENSION:
Man at 65, Woman at 60	£90.70
† Married Man over 65 with wife under 60	£145.05
Married woman over 60 where husband in receipt of full State Retirement Pension	£54.35

† *When the wife earns more than £54.65 a week after expenses, including any occupational pension, the husband loses the entire married portion of the State pension.*

NOTE: A married woman over 60 (with a husband under 65) who has paid some NICs may earn a small pension in her own right. If this is less than £54.35 a week, it will be topped up to this amount when her husband receives his State retirement pension.

Minimum Income Guarantee	single person	£124.05
	married couple	£189.35
JOBSEEKERS ALLOWANCE:		£60.50

INCAPACITY BENEFIT:
Long term Incapacity Benefit	£84.50
Short term Incapacity Benefit	
Under State pension age, lower rate	£63.75
Under State pension age, higher rate	£75.40
Over State pension age, lower rate	£81.10
Over State pension age, higher rate	£84.50

SEVERE DISABLEMENT ALLOWANCE: £50.55
Age-related additions: £5.70, £11.40 or £17.75

BEREAVEMENT PAYMENT: (Lump sum)   £2,000.00

BEREAVEMENT ALLOWANCE
From age 45 for 52 weeks only from £27.21 at 45 to £90.70 at 55.

INCOME SUPPORT: 2008

The first £3,000 of savings is ignored, £6000 if you or your partner are aged 60 or over. Savings over £8,000 means normally you cannot get Income Support (16,000 if you or your partner is 60 or over.)

For more information see Leaflet IS 1 or visit www.DWP.gov.uk.

Personal allowance	Single	£60.50
	Couple	£94.95
Premiums: Pensioner *(age 60-74)*		
	Single	£63.55
	Couple	£94.40
Enhanced pensioner *(age 75-79)*		
	Single	£63.55
	Couple	£94.40
Higher pensioner *(age 80+, or 60 + if on a disability benefit)*		
	Single	£63.55
	Couple	£94.40

CHRISTMAS BONUS £10.00

FUEL BILLS
To help pensioners fund heating costs, the Goverment has authorised a fuel payment of £250 for every pensioner household, £400 if aged 80 and over.

CARERS ALLOWANCE £50.55

ATTENDANCE ALLOWANCE: *(for over 65s)*

Higher rate (day & night)	£67.00
Lower rate (daytime only)	£44.85

DISABILITY LIVING ALLOWANCE: *(claimed before 65)*

Mobility component	higher rate	£46.75
	lower rate	£17.75
Care component	higher rate	£67.00
	middle rate	£44.85
	lower rate	£17.75

For more information

Pensions Advisory Service (OPAS), 11 Belgrave Road, London SW1V 1RB. Tel: 0845 6012923.
Email: enquiries@opas.org.uk
Website: www.opas.org.uk

Pensions Ombudsman, address as above. Tel: 020 7834 9144.
Email: enquiries@pensions-ombudsman.org.uk
Website: www.pensions-ombudsman.org.uk

OPRA Pension Schemes Registry, PO Box 1NN, Newcastle upon Tyne NE99 1NN.
Tel: 0191 225 6316.

INVESTMENTS

Association of Investment Trust Companies, 9th Floor, 24 Chiswell Street, London EC1Y 4YY. Tel: 020 7282 5555.
Email: enquiries@aitc.co.uk
Website: www.aitc.co.uk

Investment Management Association, 65 Kingsway, London WC2B 6TD. Tel: 020 7831 0898.
Website: www.investmentfunds.org.uk

IFA Promotion Limited, 2nd Floor, 117 Farringdon Road, London EC1R 3BX. Tel: 020 7833 3131.
Consumer Helpline: 0800 085 3250
Email: contact@ifap.org.uk
Website: www.ifap.org.uk

Financial Services Authority (FSA), 25 The North Colonade, Canary Wharf, London E14 5HS. Tel: 020 7066 1000.
Website: www.fsa.gov.uk

SECOND HAND LIFE POLICIES

Association of Policy Market Makers, 1 Kings Court, Bath
BA1 1ER. Tel: 0845 833 0086.
Website: www.apmm.org.uk

INSURANCE

Association of British Insurers, 51/55 Gresham Street, London
EC2V 7HQ. Tel: 020 7600 3333.
info@abi.org.uk
www.abi.org.uk

British Insurance Brokers' Association, BBA House,
14 Bevis Marks, London EC3A 7NT. Tel: 0870 950 1790.
enquiries@biba.org.uk
www.biba.org.uk

See Financial Ombudsman below

BANKS & BUILDING SOCIETIES

Finacial Ombudsman Service183 Marsh Wall,
South Quay Plaza, London E14 9SR. Tel: 0845 080 1800.
Email: enquiries@financial-ombudsman.org.uk
Website: www.financial-ombudsman.org.uk

British Bankers Association, Pinners Hall,
105/108 Old Broad Street, London EC2N 1EX.
Tel: 020 7216 8800.
Website: www.bba.org.uk

National Savings & Investments, Boydstone Road,
Glasgow G58 1SB. Tel: 0845 964 5000.
Website: www.nationalsavings.co.uk

The Association of Friendly Societies, 10/13 Lovat Lane,
London EC3 8DT. Tel: 020 7397 9550.
Email: info@afs.org.uk
Website: www.afs.org.uk

STATE BENEFITS

Department for Work and Pensions – See your local telephone directory.

Retirement Pension Forcasting Team The Pension Service,
Tyneview Park, Whitley Road, Benton, Newcastle Upon Tyne
NE98 1BA. Tel: 0845 3000 168
             0191 218 7878/7777.
Email: tvp-customer-care-ba@dwp.gsi.gov.uk
Website: www.thepensionservice.gov.uk

EMPLOYMENT & SELF-EMPLOYMENT

Association of British Chambers of Commerce, 65 Petty France,
London SW1H 9EU. Tel: 0207 654 5800.
Email: info@britishchambers.org.uk
Website: www.britishchambers.org.uk

British Franchise Association Ltd, Thames View, Newtown Road,
Henley-on-Thames, Oxon RG9 1HG. Tel: 01491 578050.
Website: www.makingmoney.co.uk

Business in the Community, 137 Sheperdess Walk, London
N1 7RQ. Tel: 0870 600 2482.
Email: information@bitc.org.uk
Website: www.bitc.org.uk

Scottish Business in the Community, PO Box 408 Bankhead Ave,
Edinburgh EH11 4EX. Tel: 0131 442 2020.

Confederation of British Industry Small and Medium
Enterprise Unit, Centre Point, 103 New Oxford Street,
London WC1A 1DU.
Website: www.cbi.org.uk

Federation of Small Businesses, Sir Frank Whittle Way, Blackpool
Business Park, Blackpool FY4 2FS. Tel: 01253 336000.
Email: london@fsb.org.uk
Website: www.fsb.org.uk

National Association of Self-Employed, PO Box 2831, Burton
Joyce, Nottingham NG14 5ZR. Email: n-a-s@n-a-s.org.uk
Website: www.n-a-s.org.uk

Office of Fair Trading, Fleetbank House, 2-6 Salisbury Square,
London EC3Y 8JX. Tel: 0207 211 8000.
Email: enquires@oft.gsi.gov.uk
Website: www.oft.gov.uk

Retired Executives Action Clearing House (REACH), 89 Albert
Embankment, London SE1 7TR. Tel: 0207 582 6543.
Email: info@reach-online.org.uk
Website: www.volwork.org.uk

The Countryside Agency, John Dower House, Cresent Place,
Cheltenham, Glos. GL50 3RA. Tel: 01241 521381.
Also have 8 English Regions see Website
Website: www.countryside.gov.uk
Training and Enterprise Councils
(TECs) (Scotland Local Enterprise Council)

Training and advisory service for small and start-up businesses.
See your local phone book.

VOLUNTARY WORK

For up-to-date information of the Charities/Voluntary Organisations
throughout the UK, the following may be useful starting points:

Association of Charitable Foundations, Central House,
14 Upper Woburn Place, London WC1H 0AE.
Tel: 0207 255 4499.
Email: acf@acf.org.uk
Website: www.acf.org.uk/foundations

The Voluntary Agencies Directory (NCVO Publications)
This gives over 2500 organisations, their aims and objectives.
Address, phone/fax numbers, Email and Website. Their directory
may be available to view in your local Reference Library.
There is a Voluntary Sector HelpDesk on 0845 600 4500
(calls charged at local rates). If you are interested in becoming a
member write to The Membership Team, NCVO,
Regents Wharf, 8 All Saints Street, London N1 9RL.
Offices also in Scotland and Wales

Age Concern England, 1268 London Road SW16 6ER.
Helpline 0800 009966.
Website: www.ageconcern.org.uk

Age Concern Scotland, Causewayside House,
160 Causewayside, Edinburgh, EH9 1PR. Tel: 0845 833 0200.
Email: enquiries@ascot.org.uk

CRUSE Bereavement Care, Cruse House, 126 Sheen Road,
Richmond, Surrey TW9 1UR.

CRUSE Bereavement Care (Scotland), Suite A,
Riverview House, Friarton Road, Perth PH2 8DF.
Tel: 0131 551 1511.
Email:info@crusescotland.org.uk

Citizens Advice, Myddelton House, 115-123 Pentonville Road,
London N1 9LZ. Tel: 020 7833 2181.
Website: www.citizensadvice.org.uk

FURTHER EDUCATION

BBC Education, PO Box 1922, Glasgow, G2 3WT.
Tel: 0870 0100 0222.
Website: www.bbc.co.uk/education

Channel 4, PO Box 4000, London W3 6XJ.

Denman College (NFWI), Marcham, near Abingdon, Oxon OX13 6NW. Tel: 01865 391991.
Email: info@denman.org.uk
hq@nfwi.org.uk
Website: www.womens-institute.org.uk

Eurocentres, 56 Eccleston Square, London SW1V 1PH.
Tel: 0207 963 8450.
Website: eurocentres.com

National Extension College, 18 Brooklands Avenue, Cambridge CB2 2HN. Tel: 01223 400 200.
Email: info@nec.ac.uk
Website: www.nec.ac.uk

National Institute of Adult Continuing Education, (NAICE), Renaissance House, 20 Princess Road West, Leicester LE1 6TP.
Tel: 0116 204 4200.
Email: information@niace.org.uk
Website: www.niace.org.uk

National Open College Network, Kedleston Road, Campus University of Derby DE22 1GB. Tel: 01332 591 071.
Email: nocn@nocn.org.uk
Website: www.nocn.org.uk

Open University, Course Reservation and Sales Centre, PO Box 724, Walton Hall, Milton Keynes, MK7 6AG. Tel: 01908 274 066
Website: www. open.ac.uk/frames.html

The Third Age Trust (U3A National Office) 26 Harrison Street,
London WC1H 8JG. Tel: 020 7837 8838.
Email: enquiries@u3a.org.uk
Website: u3a.org.uk

West Dean College (The Edward James Foundation of Art,
Craft and Music), West Dean, near Chichester,
West Sussex PO18 0QZ. Tel: 01243 811301.
Email:westdean@pavillion.co.uk
Website: westdean.org.uk

Workers' Educational Association, Quick House, 65 Clifton Street,
London EC2A 4JE. Tel: 0207 426 3450.
Email: national@wea.org.uk
Website: wea.org.uk

HOLIDAYS EIL Cultural & Education Travel, 287 Worcester
Road, Malvern, Worcs. WR14 1AB. Tel: 01684 5625777.
Email: info@eiluh.org
Website: www.eiluh.org

British Institute of Florence, Palazzo Lanfredini, Lungarno
Guicciardini 9, 50125 Florence, Italy.
Website: www.britishinstitute.it

British Tourist Authority/English Tourist Board, Thames and
Tower, Black's Road, Hammersmith, London W6 9EL.

Holiday Property Bond, HPB House, 24-28 Old Station Road,
Newmarket, Suffolk CB8 8EH. Tel: 01638 660066
Website: www.hpb.co.uk

Homesitters Ltd, Buckland Wharf, Buckland, Aylesbury,
Bucks HP22 5LQ. Tel: 01296 630 730
Email: admin@homesitters/co.uk
Website: www.homesitters.co.uk

Organisation For Timeshare in Europe, Oakhouse,
Cours St Michel 100/3, B-1040, Brussels, Belgium.
Email: admin@ote-mfo.com
Website: ote-info.com

Personal record

NOTE down contact names, telephone numbers, reference numbers and other details of key documents, and keep another copy seperately. Make diary notes of renewal dates for annual insurance policies, (car/house) central heating maintenance, TV licence, subscriptions, direct debits, etc, so that you can budget effectively.

National Insurance number

Tax office/reference

Pension – current employer

Pension – past employer(s)

Life insurance company

Mortgage lender

House insurance

House contents insurance

Private health insurance

Car insurance

Driving licence details

Bank

Building society account

Credit card/s

Financial adviser

Passport number

All rights reserved; no part of this publication may be reproduced, stored in retrieval system, or transmitted in any form or by any means, electronic, mechanical, photocopying or otherwise, without the prior written permission of the publisher.